NASM Certified Personal Trainer Exam Prep

A concise study guide that highlights the information required to pass the National Academy of Sports Medicine (NASM) CPT Exam to become a certified personal trainer.

- Includes quick reference pages for Areas of Focus, Formulas & Conversions that are required for the exam.

- Includes 50 practice questions to further enhance knowledge and to have an idea of what the actual test will look like.

- Includes detailed practice question answers with explanations on how the answers were obtained.

- Includes detailed descriptions of Assessments, Nervous, Muscular, & Skeletal Systems, Nutrition, Term definitions, Training Modalities & more!

Visit our website below for additional insights or to message us with any questions you may have while preparing for your exam.

www.cptprep.com
Follow us on social @CPTPrep

Contact via e-mail at info@cptprep.com
Your feedback is welcomed and appreciated!

Table of Contents

Table of Contents

Table of Contents

NASM Certified Personal Trainer Performance Domains

Domains are listed below with percentage of questions out of the 120 multiple choice questions on the test. You are scored on 100 out of the 120 questions on the test *(20 are unscored experimental questions)*. You will have (2) hours to complete the exam. A passing score is 70 or higher on a 0 – 100 scoring scale.

Domain 1: Basic and Applied Sciences and Nutritional Concepts – 17%

Domain 2: Assessment – 18%

Domain 3: Program Design – 21%

Domain 4: Exercise Technique and Training Instruction – 22%

Domain 5: Client Relations and Behavioral Coaching – 12%

Domain 6: Professional Development and Responsibility – 10%

NASM Certified Personal Trainer Test Statistics

2016: 21,933 candidates took the test with a pass rate of 61%
(13,443 passed / 8,490 failed)

2015: 22,266 candidates took the test with a pass rate of 67%
(14,945 passed / 7,321 failed)

You can become a NASM CPT by making sure you are fully prepared come test day!

This study guide was written to help enhance the knowledge required to become a NASM Certified Personal Trainer (CPT) and to give you the confidence that you are prepared come test day. Once you become certified this guide can be used to reference important information as you begin your career as a personal trainer.

Domain Breakdown by Chapters in the NASM Manual *(Sixth Edition)*

Domain 1: Basic and Applied Sciences and Nutritional Concepts

Information for this Domain primarily comes from Chapters 1 thru 5, 17, & 18.
In this domain you will learn about the human body, the systems involved with exercise *(movement),* and their adaptation to exercise. The systems include the Nervous, Muscular, Skeletal, Cardiorespiratory, Endocrine, and Energy systems. The effects of Nutrition and Metabolism are also discussed. The study of human movement *(Kinesiology)* along with how forces affect a living body *(Biomechanics)* are covered describing the planes of motion, movement terms, types of movements, common muscle imbalances, and kinetic chain dysfunction.

Domain 2: Assessment

Information for this Domain primarily comes from Chapter 6 & 16.
This domain takes you through the process of assessing a client. The pre-assessment is the first step where you gather information about your client *(health history, exercise history, medical history, PAR-Q, and talk about their goals).* Assessments are then selected based on the needs and goals of the client. The information gathered during the initial consultation, the assessment results, and the goals of the client are then used to help design a program for your client.

Domain 3: Program Design

Information for this Domain primarily comes from Chapter 14 and part of Chapters 7 thru 13.
Program design begins with involving the client in the planning stage of the program. When a client is involved in designing their program, they are more likely to adhere to it and achieve their goals. The program must be safe, aligned with the clients goals, and based on the findings from the comprehensive assessment. Training principles are covered first so that adaptations to exercise are understood. Acute variables *(Training volume, Tempo, Resistance, Intensity, and Rest periods)* are then discussed so that programs can be modified as needed. The OPT Model *(Phase 1: Stabilization / Phase 2: Strength Endurance / Phase 3: Hypertrophy / Phase 4: Maximal Strength / Phase 5: Power)* is used to take the client through the phases based on their needs *(muscle imbalances/compensations),* fitness level, and goals. Populations with special considerations and Group training are covered here as well.

Domain Breakdown by Chapters in the NASM Manual *(Sixth Edition)*

Domain 4: Exercise Technique and Training Instruction

Information for this Domain primarily comes from Chapter 15 and part of Chapters 7 thru 13.
Integrated Fitness Training (IFT) is a comprehensive training approach that combines all of the following elements of effective movement: *Flexibility, Core, Balance, Reactive, Speed, Agility, Quickness (SAQ), and Resistance training.* Proper technique for each of the elements of IFT are found in this domain. A checklist for correct spotting technique along with a demonstration, and appropriate cueing from the personal trainer will ensure the client maintains proper position, form, technique, and control during exercise movements. Effective communication with a client depends on what type of learner they are *(Visual, Auditory, and Kinesthetic). *If a client asks you to demonstrate an exercise they are likely more of a visual learner whereas an auditory learner may ask for you to describe the exercise technique to them.* Providing the appropriate types of feedback *(Evaluative, Supportive, and Descriptive)* to the client is also important for motivation and maintaining correct exercise technique.

Domain 5: Client Relations and Behavioral Coaching

Information for this Domain primarily comes from Chapter 19.
This domain begins with building rapport with your client. Rapport begins with the first impression and continues to grow throughout the client-trainer relationship. This foundation of mutual understanding, trust, and respect increases the likelihood of your client's success with their program. Coaching and communication strategies include the following: *active listening, expressing empathy, motivational interviewing, positive affirmation, intrinsic, and extrinsic motivation.* Coaching styles and behavior change strategies such as the *Transtheoretical Model (TTM)* can be used to help the client overcome barriers and maintain adherence to exercise. Teaching clients effective goal setting techniques and types of goals *(SMART, objective, subjective, process, outcome, short-term, and long-term)* will help them set challenging but achievable goals for themselves.

Domain 6: Professional Development and Responsibility

Information for this Domain primarily comes from Chapter 20.
NASM CPT scope of practice is covered in this domain along with the continuing education requirements to maintain certification *(CEU's)*. Types of training facilities and their demographics are discussed to help you navigate the professional fitness environment and choose what path works best for you. Sales and marketing are key factors in being a successful fitness professional. Strategies are discussed to give you a blueprint for success in this area.

Domain 1: Basic and Applied Sciences and Nutritional Concepts

The following areas are covered in this domain:

- Human Body Term Definitions
- Planes & Axes of Motion
- Types of Movements
- Movement Term Definitions
- Force, Torque, and Levers
- Nervous System
- Muscular System
- Skeletal System
- Muscle Imbalances
- Kinetic Chain Dysfunction
- Cardiorespiratory System
- Nutrition
- Endocrine System
- Metabolism
- Energy Systems

Human Body Term Definitions

Kinesiology: The study of human movement.

Biomechanics: The study of how forces affect a living body. Evaluation of how the body moves.

Anatomic position: Standard posture wherein the body stands upright with the arms beside the trunk, the palms face forward, and the head faces forward.

Ground reaction force: An equal and opposite external force that is exerted back onto the body by the ground.

Qualitative analysis: Applying principles of proper technique and combining them with observations in order to make an educated evaluation. *Primary focus for the fitness professional to observe and work with clients effectively.*

Quantitative analysis: Taking physical measurements and making mathematical computations to reach a conclusion.

Anatomic Location Term Definitions

Anterior: Toward or on the front side of the body.

Posterior: Toward or on the back side of the body.

Superior: Toward the head; higher

Inferior: Away from the head; lower

Proximal: Closest from the center of the body or landmark

Distal: Farthest from the center of the body or landmark

Medial: Toward the midline of the body

Lateral: Away from the midline of the body; to the side

Contralateral: Body part located on the opposite side of the body.

Ipsilateral: Body part located on the same side of the body.

A visual representation of the anatomic locations can be found on Page 84 Figure 5.2 of NASM Essentials of Personal Fitness Training - Sixth Edition.

Planes and Axes of Motion

Sagittal plane: Divides the body into the right & left sides. Flexion and extension exercises are primarily involved in this plane. *Squats, bicep curls, triceps pushdown, walking & running are examples of movements in the Sagittal plane.*

Frontal plane: Divides the body into anterior & posterior (front / back) portions. Vertical & lateral movements occur in this plane (abduction, adduction). *Jumping jacks, overhead press, lateral raises, and windmills are examples of movements in the Frontal plane.*

Transverse plane: Divides the body into superior & inferior (top / bottom) portions. Horizontal & rotational movements take place in the transverse plane.
Trunk rotation & swinging a bat are examples of movements in the Transverse plane.

Note: The plane in which an exercise occurs is in relation to the body not the position of the body. Performing jumping jacks while standing up and making a snow angel while lying on the ground are both frontal plane movements.

Medial-lateral axis: Straight line that cuts through the body laterally side to side. In the sagittal plane, rotation happens around this axis. *A hip hinge is a movement that occurs around a medial-lateral axis.*

Anterior-posterior axis: Straight line that cuts through the body from front to back. In the frontal plane, rotation happens around this axis. *Raising an arm laterally is a movement that occurs around an anterior-posterior axis.*

Longitudinal axis: Straight line that cuts through the body from top to bottom. Rotation around a longitudinal axis takes place in the transverse plane. *Spinal rotation with twisting of the trunk is an example of a movement around a longitudinal axis.*

It helps to visualize the planes and know which movements occur in each. A visual representation of the planes and axes can be found on Page 85 Figure 5.3 of NASM Essentials of Personal Fitness Training - Sixth Edition.

Types of Movements

Open chain movements occur when a distal segment *(hand or foot)* moves in space.
Bicep Curls, Lying triceps extensions, Leg extensions & Leg curls are examples of open chain movements.

Closed chain movements occur when distal segments are fixed in place.
Push-ups, Pull-ups, Squats, Deadlift & Lunges are examples of closed chain movements.

Sagittal plane movements include flexion, extension, hyperextension, dorsiflexion, and plantar flexion joint actions.

Frontal plane movements include the following joint actions: abduction and adduction, lateral flexion at the spine, and eversion and inversion of the foot.

Transverse plane movements include the following joint actions: internal and external rotation, pronation and supination, and horizontal abduction and adduction, as well as scapular retraction and protraction.

Range of Motion (ROM) is the amount of movement produced by one or more joints.

Multijoint movements involve using two or more joints to perform the movement.

Multiplanar movements occur in more than one plane of motion.

Incorporating functional exercises that include both multijoint and multiplanar movements that mimic activities of daily living will set clients up for long-term success.

Movement Term Definitions

Supine Position: Lying face up.

Prone Position: Lying face down.

Flexion: Movement involving a decrease in joint angle.
Towards, closer

Extension: Movement involving an increase in joint angle.
Extended, away, further

Adduction: Movement toward the midline of the body, usually in the frontal plane.

Abduction: Movement away from the midline of the body, usually in the frontal plane.

Plantar flexion: Movement at the ankle joint that points the foot downward.
Like a ballerina

Dorsiflexion: Movement at the ankle joint that points the foot up towards the leg.
The foot should be dorsiflexed to ensure proper front-side mechanics during sprinting.

Inversion: Movement of the foot which causes the sole of the foot to face inwards.

Eversion: Movement of the foot which causes the sole of the foot to face outwards.

Supination of the foot: A combination of plantar flexion, inversion, and adduction.

Pronation of the foot: A combination of dorsiflexion, eversion, and abduction.

Hyperextension: Movement that extends the angle of a joint greater than normal.

Rotation: Right or left twist in the transverse plane, usually used to describe neck & trunk movement.

Circumduction: A compound circular movement involving flexion, extension, abduction & adduction, circumscribing a cone shape.

Force, Torque, and Levers

Kinetics: The study of forces.

Force: A push or pull that can create, stop, or change movement.

Force = Mass x Acceleration

Lever: A relatively rigid rod or bar that rotates around a fulcrum *(pivot point)*. There are (3) different types of lever classes where an effort or force and a resistance are applied.

1) **First-class lever**: A force is applied on one side and a resistance is applied on the other side. *A playground seesaw with someone on each end is an example. (think agonist & antagonist muscles on opposite side of a joint)*

2) **Second-class lever**: The fulcrum is toward the end of one side *(either side)*. Both the applied force and the resistance are on the same side with the resistance closer to the fulcrum *(pivot point)*. *Moving a loaded wheelbarrow is an example. *A calf raise is an example for the human body. The ball of the foot is the fulcrum, the weight of the body is the resistance, and the calf muscle applies the force.*

3) **Third-class lever**: The fulcrum is toward the end of one side *(either side)*. Both the applied force and the resistance are on the same side with the applied force closer to the fulcrum *(pivot point)*. *Using a shovel to scoop up gravel is an example. The top hand is the fulcrum as the other hand applies the force to pick up the gravel (resistance). *A dumbbell biceps curl is an example of a third-class lever.*

See Figure 5.15 on page 97 of NASM Essentials of Personal Fitness Training - Sixth Edition for diagrams showing the lever classes.

Human Movement System

The Human Movement System is comprised of the following (3) interwoven systems that allow our bodies to move: **Nervous, Muscular, & Skeletal systems.**

Nervous System

The nervous system is a conglomeration of billions of cells specifically designed to provide a communication network within the human body.

Think of the nervous system as the software that tells the hardware of the body when to move, in which direction, and at what speed. **The nervous system is the conductor and the muscles are the orchestra.**

Central Nervous System (CNS): The division of the nervous system comprising the brain and the spinal cord. Its primary function is to coordinate the activity of all parts of the body.

Peripheral Nervous System (PNS): The portion of the nervous system that is outside the brain and spinal cord *(somatic & visceral).* The primary function is to connect the central nervous system (CNS) to the limbs and organs, serving as a communication relay with the rest of the body.

Autonomic Nervous System (ANS): The part of the nervous system responsible for control of the bodily functions **not consciously directed**, such as breathing, the heartbeat, and digestive processes.

Sympathetic Nervous System (SNS): Part of the autonomic nervous system (ANS) that activates what is often termed the *"fight or flight"* response.

Parasympathetic Nervous System (PNS): Part of the autonomic nervous system (ANS) that stimulates *"rest and digestion"* physiological processes.

Neuron: The functional unit of the nervous system.
Comprised of (3) main parts: the cell body, an axon, and dendrites.

Efferent neuron: Motor neurons that send a message for muscles to contract.
They effect/cause movement.

Afferent neuron: Nerve impulses that move toward the spinal cord and brain from the periphery of the body and are sensory in nature.

Mechanoreceptors: Sensory receptors responsible for sensing distortion in body tissues.

Joint receptors: Receptors in and around a joint that respond to pressure, acceleration, and deceleration of the joint.

Proprioception: The cumulative sensory input to the central nervous system from all mechanoreceptors that sense body position and limb movements.

Neuromuscular efficiency: When the neuromuscular system allows agonist, antagonists, and stabilizers to produce muscle actions in all three planes of motion synergistically.

Altered neuromuscular efficiency: Occurs when the kinetic chain is not performing optimally to control the body in all three planes of motion.

Intermuscular coordination: The ability of the neuromuscular system to allow all muscles to work together with proper activation and timing.

Structural efficiency: The structural alignment of the muscular and skeletal systems that allows the body to maintain balance in relation to its center of gravity. *(Optimal Posture)*

Functional efficiency: The ability of the neuromuscular system to perform functional tasks with the least amount of energy, decreasing stress on the body's structure.
Functional efficiency is a result of structural efficiency.

Motor unit: The functional unit of the neuromuscular system. Consisting of the alpha motor neuron and the muscle fibers that it activates.

Motor output: Response to stimuli that activates movement in organs or muscles.

Motor control: How the central nervous system integrates internal and external sensory information with previous experiences to produce a motor response.

Motor learning: The integration of motor control processes with practice and experience that leads to relatively permanent changes in the body's capacity to produce skilled movements.

Motor development: The change in motor skill behavior over time throughout the lifespan.

Motor behavior: Motor response to internal and external environmental stimuli. The collective study of the previous (3) concepts: ***Motor control, motor learning, & motor development.***

Acetylcholine acts at the neuromuscular junction to excite the muscle fibers of a motor unit.

Muscular System

Three types of muscle: Skeletal, Cardiac, Smooth

Skeletal muscles are consciously controlled. They provide locomotion and stability to the skeletal system. These muscles are the focus of the fitness professional to help clients achieve increased skeletal muscle activation, coordination, strength, size *(hypertrophy)*, and form during movement patterns.

Muscle fiber types: Type I *(slow-twitch)*, Type IIx *(fast-twitch)*, Type IIa *(intermediate)*
*Type IIa is a hybrid with both fast twitch (explosive) & slow twitch (endurance) capabilities.

Type I characteristics: Red in color, smaller in size, produce less force, slow to fatigue, higher aerobic capacity due to a large number of capillaries, mitochondria, & myoglobin for increased oxygen delivery & usage.

Muscles that act primarily as stabilizers generally contain greater concentrations of Type I *(slow-twitch, endurance)* muscle fibers. The core muscles are an example of this as they stabilize the spine during loading and movement throughout the day. Stabilizer muscles are better suited for endurance-type training *(higher-volume, lower-intensity)*.

Type II characteristics: White in color, larger in size, produce more force, quick to fatigue, higher anaerobic capacity, and decreased oxygen delivery due to less capillaries, mitochondria, & myoglobin.

Muscles primarily responsible for joint movement generally contain greater concentrations of Type II *(fast-twitch, explosive)* muscle fibers. These muscles are better suited for strength and power-type training *(higher-intensity, lower-volume)*.

Muscle has the following (4) behavioral properties:
- *Extensibility*: The ability to be stretched or lengthened.
- *Elasticity*: The ability to return to normal or resting length after being stretched.
- *Irritability*: The ability to respond to a stimulus.
- *Ability to develop tension*

Structure of Skeletal Muscle:
- *Epimysium*: The outermost layer of the muscle, made up of connective tissue that lies underneath the fascia and surrounds the muscle.
- *Perimysium*: Connective tissue that wraps around bundles of muscle fibers called fascicles.
- *Endomysium*: The innermost layer of connective tissue that surrounds the individual muscle fibers.

The smallest contractile unit of a muscle fiber *(cell)* is called a **Sarcomere**. Sarcomeres are made up of two types of muscle protein: **Actin** *(thin filament)* & **Myosin** *(thick filament)* which slide across each other to provide muscle contraction *(sliding filament theory)*. The arrangement of myosin and actin gives the skeletal muscle its striated appearance.

Sliding-Filament Theory states that actin filaments at each end of the sarcomere slide inward on myosin filaments, pulling the Z-lines toward the center of the sarcomere and thus shortening the muscle fiber.

Relaxed Muscle Cross Section of a Sarcomere

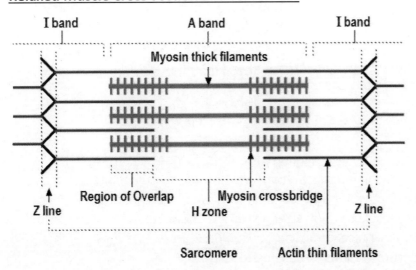

The regulation of calcium controls muscular contraction. The discharge of an ***action potential*** from a motor nerve signals the release of calcium from the sarcoplasmic reticulum into the myofibril, causing tension development in muscle.

*Calcium and ATP are necessary for cross-bridge cycling with actin and myosin filaments.

The number of cross bridges that are formed between actin and myosin at any instant in time dictates the force production of a muscle. Muscle force capability is greatest when the muscle is at its resting length due to the increased opportunity for actin-myosin cross bridges. If a muscle is contracted or stretched the force capability is reduced.

Proprioceptors are specialized sensory receptors located within joints, muscles, and tendons that provide the central nervous system with information needed to maintain muscle tone and perform complex coordinated movements.

Muscle spindles are proprioceptors that sense any stretching or tension within a muscle; their primary function is to respond to the stretch of a muscle and through a reflex action initiate a stronger muscle action *(contraction)* to reduce the stretch, called *"**Stretch reflex**."*

Golgi tendon organs (GTO) attach to the tendons near the junction of the muscle. They are proprioceptors that detect differences in tension & when excessive tension is detected they send a signal to prevent the muscle from contracting to prevent muscle injury resulting from over-contraction. GTO will signal the muscle to relax after approximately 30 seconds of applied tension to the muscle. *This is why self-myofascial release (SMR) & static stretches should be held for 30 seconds to allow the GTO to inhibit the muscle and allow the joint to be taken further into its range of motion increasing the stretch.*

*Muscle spindles (contract) muscles / Golgi tendon organs (relax) muscles

Autogenic inhibition is the process by which neural impulses that sense tension (GTO) are greater than the impulses that cause muscles to contract (muscle spindles), providing an inhibitory effect to the muscle. Activation of a Golgi tendon organ (GTO) inhibits a muscle spindle response, causing the muscle to relax after a stretch is held. An initial static stretch *(low-force)* causes a temporary increase in muscle tension *(low-grade)*. As the stretch is held a **stress-relaxation response** occurs gradually releasing tension.

Reciprocal inhibition: The simultaneous contraction of one muscle and the relaxation of its antagonist to allow movement to take place. The muscles on one side of a joint relax to allow the muscle on the other side to contract appropriately. *Agonist contract / Antagonist relax* *Biceps contract, triceps relax & vice versa.*

Length-Tension relationship (LTR): The resting length of a muscle and the tension the muscle can produce at that resting length. LTR describes the relationship between the contractile proteins *(actin & myosin)* of a sarcomere and their force-generating capacity. When these contractile proteins are ideally aligned with the most cross-bridging they can produce the greatest amount of force. Shortening or lengthening minimizes the cross-bridges reducing the muscles ability to produce optimal force. *Visualize a fighter trying to throw a punch into a heavy bag, but they are too close or too far away to land it with optimal force.*

Force-couple relationship: Muscle groups moving together to produce movement around a joint. *Altered force-couple relationships cause synergistic dominance.*

Muscle Imbalances

Musculoskeletal system: The combined, interworking system of all muscles and bones in the body.

Muscle imbalance is the alteration of muscle length surrounding a joint.

Muscle imbalances can be caused in a variety of ways:

- Postural stress
- Emotional duress
- Repetitive movement
- Cumulative trauma
- Poor training technique
- Lack of core strength
- Lack of neuromuscular efficiency

Postural distortion patterns are predictable patterns of muscle imbalances resulting from poor posture, improper movement or injury.

Muscles become dysfunctional when they are either overactive or underactive.

Overactive muscle: Referring to a state of having disrupted neuromuscular recruitment patterns that lead a muscle to be more active during a joint action. *Overactive muscles are shortened, tight, and strong.*

Underactive muscle: Referring to a state of having disrupted neuromuscular recruitment patterns that lead a muscle to be relatively less active during a joint action. *Underactive muscles are lengthened and weak.*

Altered reciprocal inhibition (altered length-tension): Process by which a short muscle, a tight muscle, and/or myofascial adhesions in the muscle cause decreased neural drive of its function antagonist. *Tight hip flexors decrease neural drive to the gluteus maximus inhibiting its function. This causes synergistic dominance where the synergist (hamstrings) takes over to perform movement.*

Synergistic Dominance (altered force-couples): When synergists take over function for weak or inhibited prime movers. *Understanding and identifying synergistic dominance will help you cue clients into better form.*

See Figures 7.4 thru 7.6 on Pages 166 and 167 of NASM Essentials of Personal Fitness Training - Sixth Edition.

Once imbalances are identified, overactive muscles should be lengthened, and underactive muscles strengthened to restore proper length-tension relationships.

Muscle Action Definitions

Concentric: Shortening portion of muscle contraction. *(Moving external resistance)*

Eccentric: Lengthening phase of muscle contraction. *(Control during lengthening portion of a movement against force)*

Isometric: Static, muscle stays in the same place against an external load. *(Joints do not move)*

Isotonic: Same tone throughout a movement.

Isokinetic: Same speed throughout a movement.

*Muscle actions involving joint movement are considered dynamic

Active Force: Muscle tension that is generated by its contractile elements.

Concentric activation: The production of an active force when a muscle develops tension while shortening in length. **Concentric means together, toward the center.*

Eccentric activation: The production of an active force when a muscle develops tension while lengthening. **Eccentric activation slows movement, "applying the brakes" to maintain control.*

Isometric activation: The production of an active force when a muscle develops tension while maintaining a constant length.

Isolated function: A muscle's primary function. A muscle action produced at a joint when a muscle is being concentrically activated to produce an acceleration of a body segment.

*Learn a muscles concentric muscle action to remember its isolated function. The biceps contract to flex the elbow joint. *Perform the movements to help memorize muscle function.

Eccentric function: Action of a muscle when it is generating an eccentric contraction. **Incorporating exercises that challenge a muscles eccentric function may help prevent injury during many functional movements.*

Integrated function: The coordination of muscles to produce, reduce, and stabilize forces in multiple planes for efficient and safe movement. **Inclusive of all muscle functions (concentric, isometric, eccentric).*

Muscle Term Definitions

Agonist: Muscles that work as the prime mover during movement / joint action.
*Biceps are agonist during a bicep curl. *Agonist perform concentric activation.*

Antagonist: Muscles that oppose the prime mover during movement / joint action.
*Triceps are antagonist during a bicep curl. *Antagonist perform eccentric activation.*

Synergist: Muscles that assist the prime mover during movement / joint action.
Synergist help the prime movers perform more efficiently.

Stabilizer: Muscles that minimize unwanted movement while the agonist and synergists work to provide movement at the joint. *The core muscles are stabilizers in all movement.*

Hypertrophy: Increase in size of muscle fibers

Hyperplasia: Increase in number of muscle fibers

Atrophy: Decrease in muscle fibers

DOMS: Delayed Onset Muscle Soreness

Location and Function of Muscles

Origin: The relatively stationary attachment site where skeletal muscle begins.

Insertion: The relatively mobile attachment site.

Muscle belly: The mid-region in between the origin and insertion.

Line of pull: The direction in which a muscle is pulled.

Parallel muscle: Muscle with fibers that are oriented parallel to that muscle's longitudinal axis.
The rectus abdominis (abs) run parallel to their origin and insertion points.

Pennate muscle: Muscle with fibers that are oriented at an angle to the muscle's longitudinal axis. *Like a feather, it fans out from the origin & insertion. The calf muscle is an example.*

Tendons: Connective tissues that attach muscle to bone and provide an anchor for muscles to produce force.

A **monoarticulate** muscle crosses one joint. A **biarticulate** muscle crosses two joints.

Muscle Locations by Area of the Body

Rotator cuff: Supraspinatus, Infraspinatus, Teres minor, Subscapularis (**SITS**)

- *Supraspinatus*: Abducts the glenohumeral (shoulder) joint
- *Infraspinatus*: Externally rotates the glenohumeral (shoulder) joint
- *Teres minor*: Externally rotates the glenohumeral (shoulder) joint
- *Subscapularis*: Internally rotates the glenohumeral (shoulder) joint

Neck: Levator Scapulae, Sternocleidomastoid, Scalenes, Longus Coli, Longus Capitis

Shoulder / Chest (Anterior): Pectoralis Major & Minor, Anterior Deltoid, Medial Deltoid, Serratus Anterior

Shoulder / Back (Posterior): Upper, Middle, & Lower Trapezius, Rhomboid Major & Minor, Posterior Deltoid, Teres Major

Arms: Biceps Brachii, Triceps Brachii, Brachioradialis, Brachialis

Back: Superficial Erector Spinae (Iliocostalis, Longissimus, Spinalis), Quadratus Lumborum, Multifidus, Latissimus Dorsi

Core (Abdominal): Rectus abdominis, Internal & External Oblique, Transverse Abdominis, Diaphragm

Hip: Adductor Longus, Adductor Magnus (anterior & posterior fibers), Adductor Brevis, Gracilis, Pectineus, Gluteus Medius, Gluteus Minimus, Gluteus Maximus, Piriformis, Tensor Fascia Latae (TFL), Iliacus, Psoas, Sartorius

Hip flexor complex: Iliacus, Psoas, Sartorius, Rectus Femoris, Pectineus, Tensor Fascia Latae

Quadriceps: Vastus Lateralis, Vastus Intermedius, Vastus Medialis, Rectus Femoris

Hamstring complex: Biceps Femoris (long & short heads), Semimembranosus, Semitendinosus

Lower Leg (Anterior/front): Anterior Tibialis, Peroneus Longus

Lower Leg (Posterior/Calf): Posterior Tibialis, Soleus, Gastrocnemius

*Visual representations of the muscles and locations can be found in Appendix D from Pages 623 – 644 of NASM Essentials of Personal Fitness Training - Sixth Edition.

Muscles of the Core		
Local Stabilization System	**Global Stabilization System**	**Movement System**
Transversus abdominis	Quadratus lumborum	Latissimus dorsi
Internal oblique	Psoas major	Hip flexors
Lumbar multifidus	External oblique	Hamstring complex
Pelvic floor muscles	Portions of internal oblique	Quadriceps
Diaphragm	Rectus abdominis	
	Gluteus medius	
	Adductor complex * Adductor magnus * Adductor longus * Adductor brevis * Gracilis * Pectineus	

Local Stabilization System: The local core stabilizers are muscles that attach directly to the vertebrae. They consist of primarily Type 1 *(slow twitch)* muscle fibers with a high density of muscle spindles. Their main function is to provide support and stabilization of the spine. They also aid in proprioception and postural control.

Global Stabilization System: Comprised of muscles that attach from the pelvis to the spine. These muscles provide stability between the pelvis and spine, act to transfer load between the upper and lower extremities, and provide stabilization and eccentric control during functional movements.

Movement System: Comprised of muscles that attach the spine and/or pelvis to the extremities. These muscles are primarily responsible for concentric force production and eccentric deceleration during dynamic movement.

These three muscular systems work together to provide dynamic stabilization and neuromuscular control of the entire core (LPHC).

Lumbo-Pelvic-Hip-Complex (LPHC): Involves the anatomic structures of the lumbar and thoracic spines, the pelvic girdle, and the hip joint.

These systems should be trained in the proper order starting with Stabilization then progressing to the Global stabilization and Movement systems. A solid foundation of stability must be built in order to move efficiently.

Skeletal System

The skeletal system serves the following (5) major roles in the body:

- **Movement**: The skeletal system consists of levers *(bones)* and pivot points *(joints)* the muscular system acts upon to create movement.
- **Support**: Bones are the framework of the body that everything else is built on top of or held within.
- **Protection**: Bones encase vital organs and protect them from trauma. The skull protects the brain, and the rib cage protects the heart & lungs.
- **Blood production**: Blood cells are formed in the bone marrow which is housed in the cavity of certain bones in the body.
- **Mineral storage**: Minerals such as calcium and phosphorus are stored in bones.

Axial Skeleton: Portion of the skeletal system that consists of the bones of the skull, rib cage, and vertebral column. *Composed of 80 bones*

Appendicular Skeleton: Portion of the skeleton that includes the bones that connect to the spinal column including the upper extremities and lower extremities. *Composed of 126 bones*

The bones of the skeletal system are categorized into (5) major categories: Long bones, short bones, flat bones, irregular bones & sesamoid bones. *Bones are living tissues in the body that adapt and become stronger to weight-bearing exercise. (increased bone mass, density & strength)*

Epiphysis: The end of the long bone, the primary site for bone growth, involved in red blood cell production.

Diaphysis: The shaft portion of a long bone.

Curves of the spine: Cervical, Thoracic, Lumbar, And Sacral

- **Kyphosis**: Primary curves *(thoracic / sacral)*
- **Lordosis**: Secondary curves *(cervical / lumbar)*
- **Scoliosis**: Lateral deviation of the spine in the frontal plane.
- **Hyperkyphosis or Hyperlordosis**: Deviations of the spine in the sagittal plane

There are **24** individual **vertebrae** in the spine:

- **7** Cervical (Neck)
- **12** Thoracic (Mid-back) *Ribs are connected to these*
- **5** Lumbar (Low-back)

We eat breakfast at 7, lunch at 12 and dinner at 5 is a good way to remember the vertebrae.

Types of Joints

Nonsynovial joints: Joints that do not have a joint cavity, connective tissue, or cartilage. *Found in sutures of the skull.*

Synovial joints: Joints that are held together by a joint capsule and ligaments; they are most associated with movement in the body. *They comprise 80% of all joints in the body.*

Types of Synovial joints: Hinge, gliding, condyloid, saddle, pivot, & ball-and-socket.

Hinge joints are formed between two or more bones where the bones can only move along one axis to flex or extend. *Ankle, Elbow & Knee joints are examples of hinge joints.*

Ball-and-Socket is a type of synovial joint where the ball-shaped surface of one bone fits into a cup-like depression of another bone. These joints are capable of moving on multiple axes from the common center of the ball joint. *Hip & Shoulder (Glenohumeral) joints are examples of ball & socket joints.*

Arthrokinematics: The motions of the joints in the body. *The three major motions are roll, slide, and spin.*

Arthrokinematic dysfunction *(altered joint motion)*: Caused by altered length-tension relationships and force-couple relationships that affect the joints and leads to abnormal joint movement *(arthrokinematics)* and proprioception causing poor movement efficiency.

Tendons link muscle & bone / *Ligaments* link bone to bone

Tendons and ligaments have a low blood supply which is why they are slower to heal from injury and take longer to adapt to exercise-induced stresses, compared to muscles.

Cardiorespiratory System

The **cardiorespiratory system** is composed of the cardiovascular and respiratory systems.

Cardiovascular system: System of the body composed of the heart, blood, and blood vessels.

Respiratory system: System of the body composed of the lungs and respiratory passages that collect oxygen from the external environment and transport it to the bloodstream.

Kinetic Chain Dysfunction

Kinetic chain: The combination and interrelation of the actions of the nervous, muscular, and skeletal systems to create movement.

Kinetic chain movement demonstrates how moving one joint in the body affects the others. All joints in the body are linked together *(like a chain)*. If one joint is not working properly, it will affect other joints and increase the potential for injury. Fitness professionals should aim to restore efficient and functional movement patterns in their clients.

There are (5) major kinetic chain checkpoints:
- Foot & ankle
- Knee
- Lumbo-pelvic-hip complex (LPHC)
- Shoulder girdle
- Head (cervical spine)

*Every movement should be checked for alignment through the (5) kinetic chain checkpoints.
*Ask clients probing questions to find out where their activities of daily living can possibly cause kinetic chain dysfunctions (such as sitting at a desk in slouched position).

The kinetic chain has tensional integrity *(tensegrity)* in which compression and tension of the bones, joints, and soft tissues give the body its form *(structure)*. Tensegrity provides stability and efficiency during static states and dynamic movements.

The (3) major causes of kinetic chain dysfunction are **repetitive movement**, **suboptimal positioning**, and /or frequent **lack of movement**. **Injuries can also cause kinetic chain dysfunction.*
- **Pattern overload**: Repetitive physical activity that moves through the same patterns of motion, placing the same stresses on the body over time.

- **Suboptimal positioning**: Less than optimal positioning that when repeated reinforces poor motor patterns and can lead to abnormal stress and pattern overload.

- **Repetitive lack of motion**: Frequent immobility, which holds the potential for repetitive stress injuries.

Repetitive stress injury (RSI): Injury due to pattern overload.

Cumulative injury cycle: A cycle whereby an injury will induce inflammation, muscle spasm, adhesions, altered neuromuscular control, and muscle imbalances. Muscle imbalance can lead to more inflammation, and the cycle repeats.

Hypermobility: Decrease in normal movement and functionality of a joint, which affects the range of motion.

Shoulder impingement: When the space between the bone on top of the shoulder (acromion) and the tendons of the rotator cuff rub against each other during arm elevation.

The Heart

There are four chambers of the heart: Right Atrium, Right Ventricle, Left Atrium, and Left Ventricle. *Think of these chambers as two separate pumps with two champers in each. *The ventricles "pump" the blood & the atriums "collect" the blood.*

The right atrium is responsible for collecting deoxygenated blood coming from the body, and the right ventricle pumps this blood through the lungs. The left atrium receives the oxygenated blood from the lungs, and the left ventricle pumps it to all parts of the body.

Blood flows through the heart chambers in the following order:
Right Atrium, Right Ventricle, Left Atrium, Left Ventricle

In addition to the heart chambers, there are also four heart valves that maintain blood flow in a single direction. Blood flows through the valves in the following order:

- **Tricuspid Valve**: Prevents backflow of blood into the right atrium.
- **Pulmonic Valve**: Prevents backflow of blood into the right ventricle.
- **Mitral (Bicuspid) Valve**: Prevents backflow of blood into the left atrium.
- **Aortic Valve**: Prevents backflow of blood into the left ventricle.

For a visual representation of the circulatory system see Figure 3.5 on page 60 of NASM Essentials of Personal Fitness Training - Sixth Edition.

The Sinoatrial (SA) node is the pacemaker of the heart. A specialized area of cardiac tissue located in the right atrium of the heart where the electrical impulses which determine the heart rate originate.

The Atrioventricular (AV) node is responsible for delaying the electrical impulses from the SA node for approximately 0.12 seconds between the atria & the ventricles. This allows the right & left atriums to contract & fill with blood. After a brief pause, the electrical impulse moves through the heart bundle branches to contract the right & left ventricles at approximately the same time.

Blood provides the following (3) functions: Transportation, Regulation, and Protection.

For a description of each function see Table 3.1 on page 59 of NASM Essentials of Personal Fitness Training - Sixth Edition.

Blood vessels are hollow tubes that allow blood to be transported from the heart, throughout the body, and back to the heart, creating a closed circuit. There are (3) major types of blood vessels:

- *Arteries*: Carry blood *away* from the heart. As arteries get further away from the heart they become smaller and form small terminal branches called arterioles, which end in capillaries
- *Capillaries*: The capillaries are the smallest blood vessels and the site of water and gas exchange between blood and tissues.
- *Veins*: Carry blood toward the heart. Other small vessels, called venules, collect blood from capillaries. The venules progressively merge with other venules to form veins.

Heart Rate (HR)

Normal resting heart rate is between 60-100 BPM *(Beats per Minute)*.
The average resting heart rate is 70-80 BPM.
Bradycardia: A heart rate that is slower than 60 BPM.
Tachycardia: A heart rate that is faster than 100 BPM.

Resting heart rate (RHR) is the number of contractions of the heart occurring in 1 minute while the body is at rest.*True RHR is measured just before a person gets out of bed in the morning.*

RHR is influenced by fitness status, fatigue, body composition, body position, digestion, drugs and medication, alcohol, caffeine, and stress. ***Note** certain drugs, medications and supplements can directly affect RHR. Clients should abstain from taking non-prescription stimulants or depressants for at least 12 hours prior to measuring their RHR.*

A person with a lower resting heart rate may indicate a higher fitness level. An increase in stroke volume as a result of cardiovascular adaptations to exercise reduces the heart rate. Higher resting heart rates are indicative of poor physical fitness.

Taking a 5 day average of RHR each morning and will provide a client's true RHR. Knowing a client's resting heart rate (RHR) provides insight into target heart rates for training and **signs of overtraining** when their **RHR is elevated more than 8 BPM** *(when pulse is taken in fitness setting).* If the client's heart rate is more than 8 BPM *(beats per minute)* higher than their average RHR, it is advised that the client take the day off from training.

Max Heart Rate (MHR): 220 – Age = MHR or 208 – (0.7 x Age) = MHR
e.g. 30 year old would have Max HR of 190 BPM | 220 – 30 = 190 BPM

Heart Rate Reserve (HRR): Max HR – Resting HR = HRR
e.g. 30 year old with resting HR of 60 BPM | 190 - 60 = 130 BPM

Target Heart Rate (THR) = HRR x % Intensity + Resting HR **(Karvonen Formula)**
e.g. 30 year old mentioned above to train at 80% intensity | 130 x 0.80 + 60 = 164 BPM (THR)

Blood Pressure (BP)

Blood pressure is the result of the amount of blood pumped from the heart *(cardiac output)* and the resistance the flow of blood meets at the vessels. **Blood pressure is defined as the pressure of the circulating blood against the walls of the blood vessels.**

Systolic blood pressure (SBP) is the pressure exerted on the arteries during the contraction phase of the heart *(when the heart beats)*

* SBP increases in a linear fashion with exercise intensity. A SBP that fails to rise or falls with increasing workloads may signal a plateau or decrease in cardiac output (Q).

Diastolic blood pressure (DBP) is the pressure exerted on the arteries during the relaxation phase of the heart *(in between beats)* ***Diastolic BP** is **determined** when the pulse **fades away.***

* DBP may decrease slightly or remain unchanged with exercise intensity.

The average value for systolic & diastolic blood pressure is 120/80 mm Hg *(measured in millimeters of mercury)*

Hypertension (high blood pressure) is when systolic & diastolic blood pressure meets or exceeds 140/90 mm Hg at rest.

Stroke Volume (SV)

Stroke volume is the amount of blood ejected from the left ventricle of the heart in a single contraction. SV is lower in an upright posture *(standing up)* in untrained individuals compared to trained individuals. SV also increases in the supine or prone positions *(lying down)*.

During dynamic exercise, SV increases curvilinearly with intensity. SV reaches near maximal levels approximately at 40% to 50% of maximum aerobic capacity. Once SV reaches its maximum levels, the increase in oxygen demand is met by increasing the heart rate.

Cardiac Output (Q)

Cardiac output measures the overall performance of the heart. It measures the amount of blood pumped by the heart per minute in liters using the following formula:

Heart Rate (HR) x Stroke Volume (SV) = Cardiac Output (Q)

* Cardiac output (Q) increases in a linear fashion with exercise intensity.

Nutrition

There are 6 classes of nutrients: Carbohydrates, Fats, Protein, Vitamins, Minerals & Water

Macronutrients: Carbohydrates, Fats & Protein *These are the energy sources for our body*

Micronutrients: Vitamins & Minerals

Fat soluble nutrients: Vitamins A, D, E & K

Water soluble nutrients: Vitamins B, C & Niacin

Minerals: Calcium, Phosphorus, Magnesium, Iron, Zinc, Copper, Selenium, Iodine, Fluoride, Chromium, Sodium, & Potassium

Nutrient density: The nutrient content of a food relative to its calories.

Vitamins & minerals should primarily come from eating a healthy diet with lots of vegetables, fruits, whole grains, dairy, and lean meats rather than relying on supplements such as a multivitamin to provide the recommended amounts.

Kilocalorie (Calorie) Breakdown

Fat = 9 calories per gram
Protein = 4 calories per gram
Carbohydrates = 4 calories per gram
Alcohol = 7 calories per gram
3500 kcal (calories) = 1 pound of fat

Daily Macronutrient Recommendations

Carbohydrates: (45% - 65% of total calories)
The general population should have around 3 grams per kilogram of body weight per day, those that exercise more than an hour a day 4-5 g per kg, and high-intensity exercisers 8-12 g per kg
Most, if not all of carbohydrate intake should come from complex carbohydrates.

Protein: (10% - 35% of total calories)
0.8 grams per kilogram of body weight per day for the general population.
Adult athletes can range from 1.2 to 1.7 g per kg of body weight.

Fats: (20% to 35% of total calories)
Less than 10% of fat calories should come from saturated fat

Scope of Practice

Fitness professionals can and should share general nonmedical nutrition information with their clients. Fitness professionals can have informed discussions on nutrition with their clients but never prescribe meal plans or supplements as it is outside of the scope of practice.

Carbohydrates

Complex carbohydrate: A carbohydrate with more than 10 carbon/water units. Includes the fiber and starch found in whole grains and vegetables.

Simple carbohydrate: A carbohydrate with fewer than 10 carbon/water units. Includes glucose, sucrose, lactose, galactose maltose, and fructose.

Monosaccharides are made up of a singular sugar unit and include the following:
- *Glucose (blood sugar):* A simple sugar manufactured by the body from carbohydrates, fat, and (to a lesser extent) protein that serves as the body's main source of fuel.
- *Fructose:* Known as the fruit sugar, found in fruits, honey, syrups, and certain vegetables.
- *Galactose (part of lactose):* Combines with glucose and lactose.

Disaccharides are made up of two sugar units and include the following:
- *Sucrose (table sugar):* A molecule made up of glucose and fructose.
- *Lactose:* A sugar present in milk that is composed of glucose and galactose.
- *Maltose:* Sugar produced in the breakdown of starch. Rare in our food supply.

High-fructose corn syrup (HFCS) is a sweetener made from cornstarch and converted to fructose in food processing.

Glycogen is the storage form of glucose that is found in the liver & muscle tissues. When carbohydrate energy is needed, glycogen is converted into glucose for use by the muscle cells.

Glucose is a simple sugar that is the preferred energy source for the human body. It is a compound of many carbohydrates. Some carbohydrates *(glucose)* are required for the oxidation *(burning)* of fat & also help keep protein *(muscle tissue)* from being broken down. However, too much glucose *(carbs/sugar)* causes an excessive insulin response that encourages the production of fat. **Glycemic index** is a measure of how carbohydrates affect blood sugar levels. Low glycemic foods help maintain glucose *(blood sugar)* levels that in turn maintains insulin balance which helps to keep the body out of the *"fat storing"* state. Blood glucose reaches peak an hour after a meal & returns to normal 2 hours after that, therefore eating every 2-4 hours helps avoid mental & muscle fatigue.

Dietary fiber is a carbohydrate that cannot be digested but aids in lowering fat & cholesterol absorption. Dietary fiber also improves blood sugar control. Since dietary fiber is non-digestible, it is subtracted from the total carbohydrate amount of a given food.

*If a food has 22 grams of total carbohydrates with 12 grams of dietary fiber then it has 10 grams of net carbs.

Fats

Lipids: A group of compounds that includes fatty acids, triglycerides *(fats and oils)*, phospholipids, and sterols such as cholesterol. Lipids are substances that are insoluble in water.

Saturated fat: A chain of carbons that are saturated with all of the hydrogens that it can hold; there are no double bonds.

Unsaturated fatty acids: Fatty acids that have areas that are not completely saturated with hydrogens, and therefore have double bonds where the hydrogen is missing.

Polyunsaturated: Fatty acids that have several spots where hydrogens are missing.
Helps lower blood cholesterol levels

Monounsaturated: A fatty acid with just one missing hydrogen.
Helps lower blood cholesterol levels while maintaining HDL

Consuming polyunsaturated & monounsaturated *"healthy fats"* along with regular exercise has been shown to improve lipid profiles. Regular exercise also helps to reduce LDL cholesterol.

Omega-3 fatty acids: Fatty acids that have anti-inflammatory effects and help to decrease blood clotting.

Omega-6 fatty acids: Fatty acids that promote blood clotting and cell membrane formation.

High-density lipoproteins (HDL): Carry lipids away from storage into the liver for metabolism and /or excretion. They are considered *"good cholesterol."*

Low-density lipoproteins (LDL): The major carrier of cholesterol & other lipids in the blood.
Can accumulate on artery walls

Triglyceride: The chemical or substrate form in which most fat exists in food and in the body.

Long chain fatty acids: Contains 14 or more carbon atoms

Medium chain fatty acids: Contains 8-12 carbon atoms

Medium chain triglycerides (MCT) are an excellent source of fuel for the body.

Short chain fatty acids: Contains 6 or less carbon atoms

Protein

Protein: Long chains of amino acids linked by peptide bonds. Serve several essential functional roles in the body. ***Protein strands are broken down in the stomach.***

Complete protein: A protein that provides all of the essential amino acids in the amount the body needs and is also easy to digest and absorb; also called *high-quality protein*. *Found in meats, eggs, dairy products, hemp seeds, and the vegetable protein in soy.*

Incomplete protein: Food that does not contain all of the essential amino acids in the amount needed by the body. *Found in beans, legumes, grains, and vegetables.*

Complementary proteins: Consuming two or more incomplete proteins together to provide needed amino acids. *People who do not eat meat and dairy products can do this to get all of the essential amino acids.*

Consuming a high-protein diet in excess of what the body can use for repair/building purposes will cause the kidneys to work harder to eliminate the increased urea produced.

Amino acids: The building blocks of proteins; composed of a central carbon atom, a hydrogen atom, an amino group, a carboxyl group, and an R-group.

There are **20 amino acids** found in the human body, **8 essential, 10 nonessential & 2 semi-essential.**

The body cannot produce essential amino acids so they must be obtained from the foods we eat whereas nonessential amino acids can be produced by the body.

Semi-essential amino acids: Arginine and histidine are considered semi-essential because the body cannot manufacture them at a rate that will support growth *(especially in children).*

Amino Acids		
Essential	**Nonessential**	**Semiessential**
Isoleucine	Alanine	Arginine
Leucine	Asparagine	Histidine
Lysine	Aspartic acid	
Methionine	Cysteine	
Phenylalanine	Glutamic acid	
Threonine	Glutamine	
Tryptophan	Glycine	
Valine	Proline	
	Serine	
	Tyrosine	

Fluid and Hydration

The human body is made up of 40% to 70% water. Most of the water in the human body (70%) is stored in the muscle tissues. Water helps to transport nutrients, rid the body of waste, regulate body temperature, lubricate joints, cushion vital organs, provides structure to the skin and body tissue.

Recommended Water Intake	
Gender or Exercise Status	Recommended Intake
Women	2.7 L (91 ounces) per day
Men	3.7 L (125 ounces) per day
2 hours pre-exercise	14-20 ounces
15 minutes pre-exercise	16 ounces, if tolerated
During exercise	4-8 oz. every 15-20 minutes or 16-32 ounces every hour
Post exercise	50 ounces for every kilogram (2.2 pounds) of body weight lost

A good indicator of hydration is urine color. When optimally hydrated urine should be a near clear pale yellow, darker colored urine indicates a state of dehydration. Proper hydration during exercise produces the following benefits:
- A less pronounced increase in heart rate
- A less pronounced increase in core body temperature
- Improvement in cardiac stroke volume & cardiac output
- Improvement in skin blood flow (*enabling better sweat rates & improved cooling*)
- Maintenance of better blood volume
- A reduction in net muscle glycogen usage (*improving endurance*)

Dehydration affects the body's ability to cool itself with sweat and leads to overheating, often compounded with a severe loss of electrolytes. Severe dehydration can lead to heat stroke. Signs of dehydration include the following: *Dry mouth, Dry skin, Headache, Rapid heartbeat, Rapid breathing, Fever, Thirst, Decreased urine output, Sleepiness or tiredness, Dizziness, Sunken eyes, Low blood pressure, Constipation, Delirium, and Unconsciousness.*

Electrolytes: Minerals in blood and other body fluids that carry an electrical charge. Minerals include *potassium, sodium, calcium, chloride, magnesium, and phosphate.* Sodium and potassium are the most important electrolytes depleted with sweat. They are commonly found in sports drinks to help replace what is lost during exercise. Electrolyte replacement is most important with prolonged physical activity. Sports drinks are ideal for those who exercise longer than 60 minutes.

Insensible water loss is water lost through mild daily sweating and exhalation of air humidified by the lungs, as well as other minor water losses, such as secretions from the eyes, which generally go unnoticed.

Supplements

Fitness professionals should not provide guidance or advice in regards to the consumption of supplements by their clients. Supplements are not approved by the Food and Drug Administration (FDA). It's up to the manufacturers to ensure their supplements are safe & effective. The FDA will investigate and take a supplement off the market if found to be unsafe after they become available.

Any supplement claiming to raise hormone levels is either illegal or making false claims.

Whey protein: A mixture of globular proteins isolated from whey, the liquid material created as a byproduct of cheese production. *Whey is absorbed by the body quickly.*

Casein: Protein commonly found in mammalian milk. *Casein is absorbed slower by the body.*

Branched-Chain Amino Acids (BCCAs): Essential amino acids, including leucine, isoleucine, and valine, that can be used for energy directly in the muscle and do not have to go to the liver to be broken down during exercise.

Creatine is a compound made in the body but that can also be consumed in the diet, mostly from meat and fish. *Involved in the supply of energy for muscular contraction.*

HMB (beta-hydroxy-beta-methylbutyrate) is a metabolite of the essential amino acid leucine that is synthesized in the human body. Used as a supplement to increase muscle mass and decrease muscle breakdown.

Caffeine has been shown to increase endurance / performance when consumed before exercise. *(5-13 milligrams one hour prior)*

Ergogenic aids: Supplements used to benefit athletic performance or exercise.

Weight Loss

There are many factors involved in successful weight loss. In order to lose weight, an individual must burn more calories than are consumed, creating a calorie deficit. Any successful weight loss strategy must create a caloric deficit by decreasing caloric intake or increasing caloric expenditure through exercise and increasing lean body mass. Fitness professionals cannot prescribe diets but can and should guide clients towards healthy eating habits that create a caloric deficit for those who want to lose weight.

Clients who require meal plans or prescription of a specific diet should be referred to a registered dietitian.

The fitness professional can help clients achieve weight loss by increasing calorie expenditure through exercise. If a client's *only* goal is weight loss, then the fitness professional should design a program involving Phases 1, 2 & 5 of the OPT Model. Stabilization *(Phase 1)* is a must for any program, followed by Strength *(Phase 2)* and Power *(Phase 5)* which will optimize calorie burning.

Clients who are seeking weight loss should perform more complex multi-joint movements at the beginning of the session and incorporate as many multi-joint exercises as possible throughout the session. These types of exercises require the use of large muscle groups which optimize calorie expenditure.

Note Hypertrophy (Phase 3) & Maximal Strength (Phase 4) can be added for clients who want to lose weight while also building strength and hypertrophy (muscle size).

It's just as important to help clients find out *why* they eat in addition to *what* they are eating. Food intake cues can come from social or emotional forces that have nothing to do with hunger. Some individuals use food as a coping mechanism to handle stress, anger, sadness, or loneliness. Food meets nutritional needs of the body, but it cannot fulfill emotional needs. If a client is using food to cope with emotions, advise them to seek the assistance of a mental health professional to help determine the root of their emotional eating and identify new, healthy coping mechanisms.

Excess consumption of any macronutrient will cause weight gain (Carbs, Fats, Protein).

Empty calories are calories that provide little or no nutrients. The main source of empty calories comes from beverages *(sweetened coffee drinks, sports drinks, sodas, beer, etc.)*

Low-Carb Diets: The rapid weight loss seen with low carbohydrate diets primarily comes from the loss of water.

Increased Lean Body Mass

It is recommended that Stabilization *(Phase 1)*, Strength *(Phase 2)*, and Hypertrophy *(Phase 3)* of the OPT Model be utilized for lean tissue growth. Phases 1 & 2 set the foundation for muscle building in Phase 3. In order to build muscle, there must be a surplus of energy *(calories)* to support tissue growth *(more calories need to be consumed than are burned each day)*. Hypertrophy training is performed at 75% to 85% of one-rep maximum *(1RM)* for 3-5 sets with short rest periods not exceeding 60 seconds.

Improve Sports Performance

Improving sports performance requires an increase in overall proprioception, strength, and power output. This type of training can be cycled through all phases of the OPT Model depending on the clients particular needs and goals. Hypertrophy *(Phase 3)* training is not necessary to improve performance and can even hinder maximal performance. Sports typically have a progression from a *preseason*, a *competitive season*, and an *off-season*.

Endocrine System

The endocrine system is comprised of organs known as **_glands_** that secrete hormones into the bloodstream to regulate a variety of bodily functions, such as mood, growth and development, tissue function, or metabolism.

Hormones are the chemical messages that enter the bloodstream to attach to target tissues and target organs.

Target cells have hormone-specific receptors, ensuring that each hormone will communicate only with specific target cells.

Testosterone (TST) is an anabolic hormone responsible for the _building_ of tissue and plays a fundamental role in the growth and repair of tissue.

Cortisol often referred to as the _"stress"_ hormone is catabolic which means the _breaking down_ of tissue. Chronic stress from overtraining, excessive stress, poor sleep, and inadequate nutrition can elevate cortisol levels leading to the following unwanted side effects:

- Breakdown of muscle tissue
- Decreased fat utilization
- Increased body composition (specifically abdominal fat)
- Decreased metabolism

Growth hormone increases the development of bone and muscle and promotes protein synthesis and fat burning; it also strengthens the immune system. Growth hormone is stimulated by the following:

- Estrogen
- Testosterone
- Deep sleep
- Hypertrophy training _(up to 23 times baseline)_
- Max strength training _(up to 3 times baseline)_

Thyroid hormones are primarily responsible for human metabolism. Triiodothyronine (T3) and Thyroxin (T4) hormones of the thyroid have been shown to be responsible for the following:

- Carbohydrate, protein, and fat metabolism
- Basal metabolic rate
- Protein synthesis
- Sensitivity to epinephrine
- Heart rate
- Breathing rate
- Body temperature

Metabolism

Metabolism is the sum of biochemical reactions that occur in the body which are required for life. It is the process by which nutrients are acquired, transported, used, and disposed of.

The digestive system consists of the following: Mouth, Stomach, Small intestine, and Large intestine.

Mitochondria: Organelle found in the cytoplasm of eukaryotic cells that contains genetic material and enzymes necessary for cell metabolism, converting food to energy. *Mitochondria are known as the powerhouses of the cell.*

Chemical energy: Energy contained in a molecule that has not yet been released in carbohydrates, fats, and proteins.

Adenosine triphosphate (ATP): Energy storage and transfer unit within the cells of the body. A high-energy compound required to do all mechanical work produced by the human body.

Metabolic pathway: A series of chemical steps or reactions that either break down or build up compounds in the body. *The body is in a constant state of breaking down & building up.*

Catabolism: A metabolic process that breaks down molecules.

Glycolysis: A catabolic process that breaks down glucose into a usable form of energy (ATP). *During glycolysis, in the presence of oxygen, pyruvic acid is converted into an important molecule in metabolism called acetyl coenzyme A.*

Anabolism: A metabolic process that builds molecules.

Protein synthesis: An anabolic process that results in the building of muscle.

Aerobic metabolism: Chemical reactions in the body that require the presence of oxygen to extract energy from carbohydrates, fatty acids, and amino acids.

Anaerobic metabolism: Chemical reactions in the body that do not require the presence of oxygen to create energy through the combustion of carbohydrates.

Lactate: A byproduct of anaerobic metabolism that occurs when oxygen delivery to the working muscles cannot meet the demands of the tissue.

First law of thermodynamics: Energy is neither created nor destroyed; rather it is transferred from one form to another. *Once energy is converted by the body into a usable form it is either used as energy (ATP), lost as body heat, or stored for future use in the form of glycogen and / or body fat.*

Energy Pathways

Muscle fibers produce ATP by three pathways: ATP Phosphocreatine (ATP-PC), Anaerobic Glycolysis & Aerobic Oxidation.

- **ATP-PC**: Used in the first 10-15 seconds at the onset of physical activity. The ATP-PC system produces energy very rapidly by utilizing the ATP stored in muscles. ATP-PC is primarily used for high power or strength type activities. *(Olympic style lifts, sprinting)*

- **Anaerobic Glycolysis:** Used in the first 2 minutes at the onset of physical activity.

- **Aerobic Oxidation**: Used during physical activity lasting longer than 2 minutes. It uses carbohydrates, fats & proteins to produce ATP.

The **Anaerobic energy systems** do not require oxygen to produce energy. They are the immediate short-term systems used in the first few minutes of exercise. *ATP Phosphocreatine (ATP-PC) & Anaerobic Glycolysis make up the anaerobic energy systems.*

The **Aerobic energy system** requires oxygen to produce energy. **The oxidative system** is used for prolonged periods of physical activity **lasting longer than 2 minutes.**

See chart of energy systems used during exercise. Figure 4.6 on page 77 of NASM Essentials of Personal Fitness Training - Sixth Edition.

Anaerobic threshold: The point during high-intensity activity when the body can no longer meet its demand for oxygen and anaerobic metabolism predominates; also called the *lactate threshold*.

Methods of Estimating Exercise Intensity

Maximal oxygen consumption (V0$_2$Max): The highest rate of oxygen transport and utilization achieved at maximal physical exertion. *Submaximal exercise test to estimate a client's V0$_2$ Max include the Rockport walk test, the step test, and the YMCA bike protocol test.*

Metabolic Energy Equivalent (MET): An index of energy expenditure. One MET is the rate of energy expenditure while at rest that is equal to an oxygen uptake of 3.5 *(V0$_2$ ÷ 3.5 = MET).*

Max Heart Rate (MHR): 220 – Age = MHR or 208 – (0.7 x Age) = MHR
e.g. 30-year-old would have Max HR of 190 BPM | 220 – 30 = 190 BPM

Heart Rate Reserve (HRR): Max HR – Resting HR = HRR
e.g. 30 year old with resting HR of 60 BPM | 190 - 60 = 130 BPM

Target Heart Rate (THR) = HRR x % Intensity + Resting HR **(Karvonen Formula)**
e.g. 30 year old mentioned above to train at 80% intensity | 130 x 0.80 + 60 = 164 BPM (THR)

Ventilatory Threshold is the point of transition between predominately aerobic energy production to anaerobic energy production. With regular exercise a person's ventilatory or lactate threshold can increase for some time beyond their primary increase in VO_2 Max. The **first ventilatory threshold (VT1)** or *"crossover"* point represents a level of intensity at which blood lactate accumulates faster than it can be cleared, which causes the person to breathe faster in an effort to blow off the extra CO_2 produced. The ***"talk test"*** *(if a person can talk comfortably in sentences while performing the exercise)* is a good indicator that someone is training below VT1. The **second ventilatory threshold (VT2)** occurs at the point of intensity where blowing off the CO_2 is no longer adequate to buffer the rapidly increasing lactate. High-intensity exercise *(≥VT2)* can only be sustained for a brief period due to the accumulation of lactate. A person's heart rate can be determined at both VT1 and VT2 thresholds by using the Submaximal talk test for VT1 and VT2 threshold testing.

VT1 & VT2 metabolic markers can be used to divide training intensity into the following 3 zones.

- Zone 1 *(low to moderate exercise)* reflects heart rates below VT1
- Zone 2 *(moderate to vigorous exercise)* reflects heart rates above VT1 to just below VT2
- Zone 3 *(vigorous to very vigorous exercise)* reflects heart rates at or above VT2

Ratings of Perceived Exertion (RPE): A technique used to express or validate how hard a client feels he or she is working during exercise.

Ratings of Perceived Exertion (RPE)	
6	No exertion at all
7	Extremely light
8	
9	Very light
10	
11	Light
12	
13	Somewhat hard
14	
15	Hard (heavy)
16	
17	Very hard
18	
19	Extremely hard
20	Maximal exertion

Domain 2: Assessment

The following areas are covered in this domain:

- Pre-Assessment Information
- Subjective Assessments
- Objective Assessments
- Static Posture Assessments
- Movement Assessments
- Common Compensations & Associated Muscle Imbalances
- Performance Assessments
- Cardiorespiratory Assessments
- Assessment Modifications for Specific Populations
- Assessment Results and Goal Planning

Pre-Assessment Information

Additional information in the following areas should be gathered during a pre-exercise interview to learn more about the client and discover potential structural issues:

- **Occupation**: Knowing a client's occupation helps determine common movement patterns that occur during their average day.

- **Extended periods of sitting**: If the client is sitting for long periods of the day then their hips are flexed for prolonged periods which can lead to tight hip flexors *(rectus femoris, tensor fascia latae, iliopsoas)* and postural imbalances.

- **Repetitive movements**: Persistent motion *(pattern overload)* that can lead to musculoskeletal injury and dysfunction.

- **Dress shoes**: Wearing shoes with high heels puts the foot/ankle in a plantar-flexed position for extended periods which can lead to postural imbalance.

- **Past injuries**: All past injuries should be discussed in order to decide whether exercise is recommended or if a medical referral is necessary. **Ankle sprains, knee injuries involving ligaments, low back injuries, shoulder injuries, and any other injuries.*

- **Past surgeries**: If not rehabilitated properly surgeries can cause pain and inflammation that can alter neural control to the affected muscles and joints.

- **Recreation**: By finding out what activities clients do outside of their work environment, the fitness professional can better design an exercise program to fit the client's needs.

Gathering this pre-assessment information will help to uncover the clients potential needs before performing any postural assessments. The client's responses can also help the fitness professional focus on specific areas when performing assessments.

Client Consultation Forms

*Below is a list of the necessary and recommended forms for the initial client consultation.

Informed consent *(assumption of risk)*

Liability waiver

Physical activity readiness questionnaire (PAR-Q)

Health-history questionnaire *(Medical history, medications & supplements, exercise history, illnesses or injuries, lifestyle information such as nutrition, stress, work, sleep, etc.)*

Exercise history and attitude questionnaire *(helps for developing goals & designing programs)*

Medical release *(if client has any condition that requires clearance for exercise)*

Testing forms *(used to record testing & measurement data during the fitness assessment)*

Client-Personal trainer agreement *(Agreement to participate)*

Assessments

Subjective assessment: Assessment used to obtain information about a client's personal history, as well as his or her occupation, lifestyle, and medical background.

Objective assessment: Assessment that addresses observations that can be directly measured and quantified by the fitness professional. *(Resting heart rate, Blood pressure, Posture and movement assessments)*

Heart Rate Sites (Pulse)
1) Radial artery *(thumb side of the wrist)*
2) Brachial *(anterior side of elbow)*
3) Carotid *(neck)*

Once the pulse is identified, count the number of beats for 10 seconds and multiply times 6 to determine the beats per minute (BPM).

*Note the **radial pulse is the preferred method when obtaining a client's pulse**. The carotid artery is not a preferred site due to the possibility of reflexive slowing of the heart rate when pressed.*

There are three methods available to determine a person's body fat: *Underwater weighing, Bioelectrical impedance, and Skinfold measurements.*

Skinfold Measurements
Use the Durnin-Womersley formula to determine body fat percentage.

Durnin formula skinfold locations: *Biceps, Triceps, Subsapular, Iliac crest.*

All skinfold measurements should be taken on the right side of the body.
See skinfold measurement locations starting with Figure 6.9 on Page 123 of NASM Essentials of Personal Fitness Training - Sixth Edition.
Add the four measurements together & see Table 6.7 on Page 124 to determine body fat %.

Body Fat Distribution: The location of fat on the body.
Waist to Hip ratio is a good indicator of body fat distribution. Waist ÷ Hip = WHR

Waist to Hip Ratio (WHR)
Waist circumference ÷ Hip circumference = Waist to Hip ratio
Health risk is high when above 0.95 for men & 0.80 for women
Health risk is high when waist circumference is ≥39.5" for men & ≥35.5" for women
Low risk is ≤31.5" for men & ≤27.5" for women

Circumference measurement locations: *Neck, Chest, Waist, Hips, Thighs, Calves, & Biceps*

Body Composition: The relative percentage of body weight that is fat versus fat-free tissue.
Current body fat targets are 15% for men and 25% for women.
*A certain amount of **essential body fat** is necessary, for men it's between 2 and 5%, and for women it is between 10 and 13%.*

Lean Body Weight (LBW): The amount of fat-free weight (mass) one has.

Body Composition Formulas

- **Lean Body Weight (LBW)** = Scale weight – Fat mass

- **Fat Weight (Mass)** = Body fat % x Scale weight

- **Desired Body Weight (DBW)** = Lean body weight ÷ (100% - Desired body fat %)

Basal Metabolic Rate (BMR): Calories burned daily without movement.
To gain or lose weight one should increase or decrease calories by 300 to 400 kcals per day.

Height & Weight Conversions
1" = 2.54 cm
1 m = 100 cm
1 Kg = 2.2 pounds

Body Mass Index (BMI): A weight to height ratio / Weight (Kg) ÷ Height (m^2)
e.g. calculate the BMI of a man who is 6ft tall & weighs 180 pounds
180 ÷ 2.2 = 81.81 Kg | 6ft x 12 = 72 inches | 72 x 2.54 = 182.88 cm | 182.88 ÷ 100 = 1.83 m
| 1.83m^2 = 3.35 | 81.81 ÷ 3.35 = 24.42 BMI

***Note**: BMI cannot determine actual body composition, which means it can unfairly categorize some individuals (e.g., someone with a lot of muscle mass could be put in "obese" category).*

Body Mass Index (BMI) Classification		
BMI	*Disease Risk*	*Classification*
<18.5	Increased	Underweight
18.6 - 21.99	Low	Acceptable
22 - 24.99	Very low	Acceptable
25 - 29.99	Increased	Overweight
30 - 34.99	High	Obese
35 - 39.99	Very high	Obesity II
>40	Extremely high	Obesity III

Posture Assessments

Static posture assessments check for proper alignment of the kinetic chain checkpoints, symmetry, and specific postural distortion patterns.

Posture: The arrangement of the body and its limbs.

Static Posture: The alignment of the body's segments, how the person holds themselves *"statically"* with no movement in space.

Dynamic Posture: The position the body is in at any moment during a movement pattern.

Stability: Characteristic of the body's joints or posture that represents resistance to change of position.

Mobility: The degree to which an articulation is allowed to move before being restricted by surrounding tissues.

__Proximal__ stability promotes __Distal__ mobility

Kinetic chain checkpoints:
- Foot & ankle
- Knee
- Lumbo-pelvic-hip complex (LPHC)
- Shoulder girdle
- Head (cervical spine)

__Note:__ When performing a static posture assessment on a client the fitness professional should focus on the obvious, gross imbalances and avoid over-analyzing minor postural asymmetries.

Trainers must work to restore and maintain client's normal joint alignment, joint movement, muscle balance, and muscle function.

The principle of *__"Straightening the body before strengthening it"__* should be a priority of the personal trainer and client early in a training program. Adhering to this principle can improve the client's efficacy in their program and increase the likelihood of success in attaining their goals.

Movement Observations & Assessments

Movement observations should relate to basic functional movements such as squatting, pushing, pulling, and balancing. Familiarize yourself with the following assessments: *Overhead Squat, Single-leg Squat, Pushing, and Pulling assessment.*

- **Overhead squat assessment**: A transitional movement assessment designed to assess dynamic flexibility, core strength, balance, and overall neuromuscular control.

- **Single-leg squat assessment**: A transitional assessment performed on one leg to assess dynamic flexibility, core strength, balance, and overall neuromuscular control.

- **Pushing assessment**: Evaluates movement efficiency and potential muscle imbalance during pushing movements.

- **Pulling assessment**: Evaluates movement efficiency and potential muscle imbalance during pulling movements.

*Know what compensations to look for and how to identify / correct overactive and underactive muscles associated.

*Additional information on these assessments can be found on Pages 139 to 150 of NASM Essentials of Personal Fitness Training - Sixth Edition.

Transitional movement assessment: A type of assessment that evaluates dynamic posture.

Knee valgus: The process where the knees move forward and in, known as *"knock knees."*

Common Compensations and Associated Muscle Imbalances

Feet turn out: The feet typically turn out due to shortened and overactive calf muscles *(soleus & lateral gastrocnemius)*. Using corrective flexibility *(stretching & SMR)* on the calves and staying away from calf raises until they have been elongated will help improve this compensation.

Knees caving in: Overactive adductors, tension fasciae latae (TFL), biceps femoris *(short head)*, and vastus lateralis *(quad muscle)* can contribute to the knees caving inward. Using corrective flexibility *(stretching & SMR)* on these muscles and avoiding adductor, abductor *(works the TFL)* and leg extension machines will help improve this compensation. Strengthening the underactive muscles *(vastus medialis oblique (VMO), medial hamstring, medial gastrocnemius, gluteus maximus and medius)* can help to further improve this compensation.

Anterior pelvic tilt (low back arches): Tight hip flexors are the prime contributor to an anterior pelvic tilt. Erector spinae *(low back)* and latissimus dorsi *(mid back)* can also be overactive. Using corrective flexibility *(stretching & SMR)* on these muscles and strengthening the hip extensors *(gluteus maximus, hamstring complex, and intrinsic core stabilizers)* will help improve this compensation. The leg press, adductor machine, leg raises, and leg extension should be avoided until proper length-tension relationships are restored at the Lumbo Pelvic Hip Complex (LPHC).

Excessive forward lean: This compensation is typically caused by shortened calves. The hip flexor complex and abdominal muscles can also be overactive while the erector spinae, gluteus maximus and medius can be underactive. Proper corrective flexibility *(stretching & SMR)* for the overactive muscles and activation exercises *(strengthening)* of the underactive muscles will help to correct this compensation.

Arms falling forward: This compensation is often caused by overactive latissimus dorsi, teres major, and the pectoral muscles of the chest. Corrective flexibility *(stretching & SMR)* should be used on the tight muscles and the following muscles should be strengthened: rhomboids, rotator cuff, mid & lower trapezius. When performing back exercise choose a wide-grip row over a narrow-grip row. Wide grip row exercises help to retract the shoulder blades and strengthen the rear delts without also strengthening the lats. Choose standing cable press over chest press machines to help stabilize the core and shoulder girdle muscles correctly.

Note: Go over these compensations multiple times so that you become familiar with the overactive & underactive muscles involved and understand ways to correct them.
See Table 7.6 on Page 196 of NASM Essentials of Personal Fitness Training - Sixth Edition.

Postural distortion patterns: Common postural malalignments and muscle imbalances that individuals develop based on a variety of factors. **There are (3) basic distortion patterns**: *Pronation distortion syndrome, Lower crossed syndrome, and Upper crossed syndrome.*

Pronation distortion syndrome: A postural distortion syndrome characterized by foot pronation *(flat feet)* and adducted and internally rotated knees *(knock knees)*.

Pronation Distortion Syndrome			
Short Muscles	*Lengthened Muscles*	*Altered Joint Mechanics*	*Possible Injuries*
Gastrocnemius	Anterior tibialis	**Increased:**	Plantar fasciitis
Soleus	Posterior tibialis	Knee adduction	Posterior tibialis
Peroneals	Gluteus maximus	Knee internal rotation	Tendonitis (shin splints)
Adductors	Gluteus medius	Foot pronation	Patellar tendonitis
Tension fasciae latae (TFL)		Foot external rotation	Low back pain
Hip flexor complex		**Decreased:**	
Biceps femoris (short head)		Ankle dorsiflexion	
		Ankle inversion	

Lower crossed syndrome: A postural distortion syndrome characterized by an anterior tilt to the pelvis *(arched lower back)*.

Lower Crossed Syndrome			
Short Muscles	*Lengthened Muscles*	*Altered Joint Mechanics*	*Possible Injuries*
Gastrocnemius	Anterior tibialis	**Increased:**	Hamstring complex strain
Soleus	Posterior tibialis	Lumbar extension	Anterior knee pain
Hip flexor complex	Gluteus maximus	**Decreased:**	Low back pain
Adductors	Gluteus medius	Hip extension	
Latissimus dorsi	Transversus abdominis		
Erector spinae			

Upper crossed syndrome: A postural distortion syndrome characterized by a forward head and rounded shoulders.

Upper Crossed Syndrome			
Short Muscles	*Lengthened Muscles*	*Altered Joint Mechanics*	*Possible Injuries*
Upper trapezius	Deep cervical flexors	**Increased:**	Headaches
Levator scapulae	Serratus anterior	Cervical extension	Biceps tendonitis
Sternocleidomastoid	Rhomboids	Scapular protraction	Rotator cuff impingement
Scalenes	Mid-trapezius	Scapular elevation	Thoracic outlet syndrome
Latissimus dorsi	Lower trapezius	**Decreased:**	
Teres major	Teres minor	Shoulder extension	
Subscapularis	Infraspinatus	Shoulder external rotation	
Pectoralis major/minor			

Performance Assessments

Performance assessments measure upper extremity stability and muscular endurance, lower extremity agility, and overall strength. The following are basic performance assessments: *Push-up test, Davies test, shark skill test, vertical jump test, 40-yard dash, pro shuttle, LEFT test, broad jump, bench press strength assessment, and squat strength assessment.*

Push-up test: Measures muscular endurance of the pushing muscles of the upper body.

Davies test: Measures upper extremity agility and stabilization.

Shark skill test: Measures lower extremity agility and neuromuscular control.

Vertical jump test: Assesses lower extremity power.

Standing broad jump: Assesses lower extremity power.

40-yard dash: Assesses acceleration and speed.

Pro shuttle test: Assesses speed, explosion, body control, and the ability to change direction *(agility)*.

LEFT test: Assesses agility, acceleration, deceleration, and neuromuscular control.

Additional information on these assessments can be found on Pages 150 to 155 of NASM Essentials of Personal Fitness Training - Sixth Edition.

Formative assessment: An informal, quick assessment of movement proficiency during a workout to gauge progress and screen for any new areas of concern.

One-Repetition Max Test

The one-rep max (1RM) test is used to determine overall upper body strength with the bench press or overall lower body strength with the squat. 1RM bench press is performed as follows:

1) Warm-up with a light resistance that can be performed easily for 8 – 10 reps
2) Take a 1-minute rest
3) Add 10-20 pounds *(5-10% of initial load)*, and perform 3-5 reps
4) Take a 2-minute rest
5) Repeat steps 3 & 4 until the **client achieves failure ideally between 3-5 reps.**
6) Use the one-rep max chart to determine the client's 1RM. *(Pages 616 - 622 of NASM text)*

Cardiorespiratory Assessments

Cardiorespiratory assessments help to identify safe and effective starting exercise intensities based on client's current fitness level. The best measurement of cardiorespiratory fitness is VO_{2Max}. However, it is not always practical to directly measure VO_{2Max}. Therefore, a submaximal test can be used to predict ones VO_{2Max}. The following are submaximal cardiorespiratory assessments:

- *YMCA 3-minute step test*
- *Rockport walk test*
- *Cycle ergometer tests*
- *Ventilatory threshold testing*

Additional information on these assessments can be found on Pages 130 to 133 of NASM Essentials of Personal Fitness Training - Sixth Edition.

Any assessment can be modified as long as the same protocols are followed each time. It is important to take note of all details and modifications while performing assessments. Compensations, movement inefficiencies and muscle imbalances that are found during an assessment should dictate whether other assessments should or should not be performed.

A client whose knees excessively adduct during squat assessments should probably not do the more advanced shark skill test due to the possible risk of injury.

Effects of Medication on Heart Rate and Blood Pressure		
Medication	*Heart Rate*	*Blood Pressure*
Beta-blockers	Decrease	Decrease
Calcium-channel blockers	Increase or No effect or Decrease	Decrease
Nitrates	Increase or No effect	No effect or Decrease
Diuretics	No effect	No effect or Decrease
Bronchodilators	No effect	No effect
Vasodilators	Increase or No effect or Decrease	Decrease
Antidepressants	Increase or No effect	No effect or Decrease

Make sure to know this table and the effects the different medications have on HR & BP.

Assessment Modifications for Specific Populations

Youth Population: Assessments for this group should be fun! The youth are still developing physically so there may be strength deficits to take into consideration. The push-up assessment can be modified by performing it on the knees or in an elevated position with hands on a bench and feet on the floor. Pushing and pulling assessments can be performed with tubing since machines are not often designed to fit the dimensions of the youth properly.

Pregnant Population: Assessment modifications for a pregnant client will depend on which trimester she is in. Generally the first trimester requires few modifications while the second and third trimesters require modifications. Explosive-type movements are not recommended in the second and third trimesters due to increased levels of relaxin, a hormone that loosens and soften ligaments. Push up assessments would need to be performed on the knees with hands on the bench. Adjustments to the overhead squat assessment may need to be modified as well due to the increased mass. The growth of the fetus can alter the woman's center of gravity *(COG)* making it more difficult to control balance, unstable assessments should be avoided or modified.

Senior Population: The senior population varies widely with some being very active in which modifications may not be necessary. Modifications are warranted in other cases where the individual is very inactive, has medical conditions, and/or taking medications. It may not be necessary to perform certain performance assessments depending on the senior client's capabilities and goals.

Obese Population: Obese individuals may not be physically capable of performing many of the common assessments and compensations can be difficult to see due to the additional mass the individuals may be carrying. The primary focus with obese clients is to decrease weight and get the individual moving. Having them perform bodyweight squats for a set amount of time *(30-60 seconds)* is a good alternative assessment to get them moving and record the number of reps performed in that timeframe to be reassessed in the future. Performing single-leg balance instead of single leg squat, modified push-up test from knees or with hands on a bench, using tubing over machines if the client does not fit comfortably on a machine, using the Rockport walk test over the YMCA 3-minute step test are all examples of modifications that can be made with the obese population.

Adjustments for Common Injuries: If a client presents a new injury the fitness professional should refer them to an appropriate medical professional. Some clients will report past injuries that they no longer experience or have addressed with physical therapy. In some cases modifications need to be made to fit the client's capabilities. Injuries often cause movement compensations in the area or connecting *(kinetic chain)* areas of the body. Someone who has experienced low back pain may show signs of a weak core by anterior & posterior tilting of the pelvis during assessments. For those with previous shoulder injuries it is important to watch for the arms falling forward during an overhead squat, and/or the shoulders elevating and head migrating forward during pushing and pulling assessments. The one-rep max bench press or push up assessment can place a large amount of stress on the shoulder complex. These assessments should be avoided or modified to decrease stress to the area.

Assessment Results and Goal Planning

When designing a program it is important for the fitness professional to focus on the obvious compensations and try not to micro analyze the client.

Common compensations seen at the foot, ankle, and knee during the overhead & single –leg squat are the feet turning out and the knees caving inward. These compensations typically occur due to lack of ankle range of motion *(especially dorsiflexion)*, weakness of the hip muscles *(hip abductors and external rotators)* or both.

Anterior tilting of the pelvis or excessive forward lean seen during the overhead squat assessment could indicate poor core control *(weak transverse abdominis, gluteals)*. Other assessments involving the core could show similar compensations *(especially in the prone position such as the push-up assessment)*.

The common compensations found can usually be addressed by improving range of motion (ROM) at the ankles, hips, and shoulders, while improving strength in the hips, core, and scapular retractors. Focusing on stretching client's calves, hip flexors, latissimus dorsi and pectorals and strengthening the gluteals, intrinsic core stabilizers, and scapular stabilizers can make considerable gains in the functional status of most clients.

*There are no set protocols for reassessments, but a general timeframe used is every 4 weeks. When a client knows they will be assessed on a monthly basis they are more likely to adhere to the program.

*Fitness professionals should assess client's movement patterns during every workout and cue them as necessary to maintain proper technique and form.

Domain 3: Program Design

The following areas are covered in this domain:

- Starting Program Design
- Session Structure and Flow
- Training Principles
- Acute Variables
- The OPT Model *(Optimum Performance Training)*
- Phase 1 *(Stabilization)*
- Phase 2 *(Strength Endurance)*
- Phase 3 *(Hypertrophy)*
- Phase 4 *(Maximal Strength)*
- Phase 5 *(Power)*
- Populations with Special Considerations
- Group Training and the OPT Model

Starting Program Design

The creation of a purposeful system or plan to achieve a goal. Involving the client in the planning stage of a program results in better adherence and completion of the program. *"Without involvement, there is no commitment"* – Stephen Covey

The fitness professional must consider the following three questions when designing a program for a client:

1) Is it safe?
2) Is it based on findings from a comprehensive assessment?
3) Does it align with the client's goals?

Exercise programs should be designed based on the client's specific movement patterns. If movement compensations and muscle imbalances are present during assessments, the program should work to correct them before performing similar movements. *If resistance is added to dysfunctional movement patterns, it increases the risk of injury and can make the compensation worse.*

Fitness professionals should aim to restore and maintain client's normal joint alignment, joint movement, muscle balance, and muscle function. The client's ability to move efficiently greatly impacts their results. Focusing on *quality* of movement over *quantity* in the initial phases will set a strong foundation to build upon in later phases of the OPT Model.

Cardio Considerations: Proper posture and form during cardio helps the body to use the correct muscles, leading to better movement, more calories burned, decreased chance of injury, and overall longevity and satisfaction with exercise.

Clients must be *mindful* of their posture while doing cardio and daily activities in order to maintain effective and efficient movements. Being self-aware of one's posture can help prevent compensations they may have from getting worse and even help to correct them over time.

Clients with feet turned out should use a *treadmill only after stretching* and/or using self-myofascial release (SMR) for overactive tight muscles and maintain a pace slow enough to keep the five kinetic chain checkpoints aligned. The use of an *elliptical trainer* is a great option for those with feet turned out because the foot pads help keep the foot straight and lower body in alignment while in use. *Versa climbers* and *Rowing machines* are also good options for those with feet turned out.

Clients with anterior pelvic tilt should follow similar protocols to the feet turned out compensation. Use of the treadmill after stretching and the elliptical trainer as long as proper form is maintained are both good options.

Clients with arms falling forward or rounded posture can perform any form of cardio as long as proper posture is maintained.

Programming / Exercise Templates are a great way for the fitness professional and client to track progress and know the when, where, how, and why they are performing specific exercises. Detailed templates help to eliminate error and let the client know what to work on during their free time when they are not with the personal trainer. It gives the client *"homework"* for lack of a better word that provides guidance and structure to their workouts.

A training template should track five items: Phase of training, Exercises used, Intensity of exercise, volume (reps x sets), and a measure of the outcome *(e.g., "great workout" or "needs improvement)*

Monthly and Yearly Templates should be created with the client and given to them so they know what to expect and the action steps needed to achieve their goals. A clients program begins with setting expectations and creating a plan to achieve the goals set. Providing these templates as part of the client's tools is essential for program adherence and success.

Examples of training templates can be found on Pages 366 to 387 of NASM Essentials of Personal Fitness Training - Sixth Edition.

Session Structure and Flow

Each exercise session should include a warm-up with SMR *(Self-Myofascial Release)* and stretching, followed by core, balance, and reactive exercises *(movement prep)*. SAQ *(Speed, Agility, & Quickness)* training should then be performed *(if appropriate)*, followed by resistance training, a cool-down, and a *"homework"* assignment *(template)* for the client.

General training session times are 30 or 60 minutes. Planning out adequate time for warm-up and cool-down within the sessions or warming up prior to the session is important. The warm-up primes the body for the conditioning phase of the session and the cool down helps to decompress from the session. Both the warm-up and cool down aid in overall flexibility, recovery, and help to mitigate potential injury.

Training sessions focus on the traditional aspect of personal training. These sessions involve learning and practicing new skills *(the physical work performed)*. The fitness professional provides motivation and cues the client during these sessions as necessary.

Coaching sessions focus on consultation. These sessions should be used to review overall performance and progress. Coaching sessions involve the fitness professional and client working together to discuss potential obstacles to success, create effective lifestyle plans, motivate the client, and create a change when necessary. Fitness professionals should ask their client's thought-provoking questions that empower the client to discover any changes that need to occur in order to achieve their goals.

Fitness coaching: The application of various behavior change and communication strategies with clients that leads to increased accountability and motivation, thus supporting their desire to achieve fitness goals.

Training Principles

General Adaptation Syndrome (GAS): (1) How the kinetic chain responds and adapts to imposed demands. (2) How the body responds and adapts to stress. GAS is broken down into the following (3) phases:

1) **Alarm phase**: The initial response to the imposed demands of exercise which last approximately 2-3 weeks. Neuromuscular adaptation is primarily taking place in this phase which can cause fatigue, weakness and soreness as the body adapts. Initial increases in strength are from the neuromuscular adaptation not actual structural, muscular changes.

2) **Adaptation phase**: The body adapts to the imposed stress of exercise by changing structures in the body (lasting approximately 4-12 weeks). During this phase muscle fibers increase in thickness and *intermuscular coordination* is improved which increases strength and the body's ability to perform the exercise movements.

3) **Exhaustion phase**: The body can no longer adapt to the imposed demands of the applied training stimulus. Further adaptations may halt and the potential for physiological and structural breakdown increases. The risk of *overtraining syndrome (OTS)* also increases.

Acute variables: The components that specify how each exercise is to be performed. *Changing the acute variables will help to ensure the body continues to experience the desired changes.*

Overload principle: In order to create physiological changes an exercise stimulus must be applied at an intensity greater than the body is accustomed to receiving. As the body adapts to a given stimulus, an increase in stimulus is required for further adaptations and improvements.

Principle of specificity: States the body will adapt to the demands that are placed upon it. *Only the muscles that are trained will adapt and change in response.*

SAID principle: Specific Adaptations to Imposed Demands

FITTE principle: Frequency, Intensity, Time, Type, Enjoyment

Principle of variation: Rationale for challenging the kinetic chain with a wide variety of exercises and stimuli.

Interval training: Training that alternates between intense exertion and periods of rest or lighter exertion.

Peripheral Heart Action System (PHA): Type of circuit training in that alternates between upper and lower body exercises throughout the circuit. PHA training keeps the blood circulating throughout the entire body during the workout preventing blood from pooling in the legs.

Periodization: Division of a training program into smaller, progressive stages.

- **Macrocycle** = *Annual plan*
- **Mesocycle** = *Monthly plan*
- **Microcycle** = *Weekly plan*

Linear periodization: Classic or traditional strength and power programming that begins with high-volume, low-intensity training and progresses toward low-volume, high-intensity training.

Linear periodization such as the OPT Model is great to use for untrained clients as it progresses them systematically thru each phase ensuring proper adaptations are met before moving to the next phase. This helps to prevent the risk of injury and overtraining.

Undulating Periodization (nonlinear): A form of periodization that provides changes in the acute variables of workouts to achieve different goals on a daily or weekly basis. A typical undulating program would follow a 14 day cycle, with three or four different workouts *(e.g., Stabilization on Monday, Strength on Wednesday, and Power on Friday)*

Overtraining syndrome (OTS): Excessive frequency, volume, or intensity of training, resulting in fatigue; also caused by a lack of proper rest and recovery.

24 to 36 total sets should be performed in a given workout to prevent overtraining.

Homeostasis: The ability or tendency of an organism or a cell to maintain internal equilibrium by adjusting its physiological processes. *When the body maintains a constant, steady state despite external changes such as exercise (physiological balance).*

Deconditioned: A state of lost physical fitness, which may include muscle imbalances, decreased flexibility, and a lack of core and joint stability.

Rhabdomyolysis: Often a sign of overtraining this condition happens when a rapid breakdown of muscle tissue results in the release of intramuscular proteins *(myoglobin, myosin protein)* into the bloodstream. This can be potentially harmful to the kidneys and could lead to kidney failure and sometimes death in extreme cases.

Valsalva maneuver: Moderate forceful exhalation against a closed glottis *(close mouth, pinch nose shut)* while pressing out as if blowing up a balloon. The Valsalva maneuver is commonly used in powerlifting to stabilize the trunk during exercises like the squat & deadlift. The Valsalva maneuver should be avoided by the general population as it increases intra-abdominal pressure, blood pressure & heart rate. This can be dangerous by hindering a person's cardiac output & cause dizziness or fainting.

Contraindicated exercise: A movement or exercise that is not recommended because it is potentially dangerous. ***Lat pulldowns with barbell behind the head is an example.***

Mechanical specificity: The weights and movements placed on the body. The specific muscular requirements using different weights and movements that are performed to increase strength or endurance in certain body parts.

Neuromuscular specificity: The specific muscular contractions using different speeds and patterns that are performed to increase neuromuscular efficiency.

Metabolic specificity: Energy demand placed on the body.

Endurance training primarily uses aerobic pathways (Aerobic Oxidation, The Oxidative System)

Strength & Power training primarily use anaerobic pathways (ATP-PC & Anaerobic Glycolysis)

Progression & Regression of Exercises

Progression of exercises: Describes the progressive stages of making an exercise more difficult or challenging. Usually by creating additional instability which enhances proprioception & neuromuscular control.

Example Progressions

- Easy to Hard
- Slow to Fast
- Static to Dynamic
- Stable to Unstable
- Simple to Complex
- Eyes Open to Eyes Closed
- Two Arms/Legs to Single-Arm/Leg
- Known to Unknown (cognitive task)
- Body Weight to Loaded Movements

Progressing an individual too quickly can lead to improper movement patterns and increase the risk of injury. A client must be able to perform an exercise with proper form and technique before progressing to a more challenging version or exercise.

Regression of exercises: Describes regressing an exercise making it easier to perform. Usually by creating a more stable base of support (i.e., both feet on the ground).

If a client is unable to perform a standard push-up you could regress the movement to have them perform it with their knees on the ground instead. Once enough strength has been built up they could progress to a traditional push-up and even further to performing push-ups with feet on a bench or stability ball.

Acute Variables

Training volume: The total amount of work performed within a specified time; typically the number of repetitions multiplied by the number of sets in a training session.

Tempo: The amount of time that a muscle is actively producing tension during exercise movements.

Repetition Tempo refers to the speed with which each repetition is performed. Tempos are listed in seconds as *(eccentric portion / isometric (pause) / concentric portion)*.

*Exercises don't have to follow the sequence listed. (Squats start with eccentric / Deadlifts start with concentric) but they are always recorded the same way starting with the eccentric portion.

Tempos for each phase of the OPT Model		
Tempo	*Adaptation*	*Phase*
Slow (4/2/1)	Stabilization, Endurance	1, 2
Moderate (2/0/2)	Strength	2, 3, 4
Fast (X/X/X)	Max strength, Power	4, 5

Load: The amount of weight lifted or resistance used during training.
*As the **load** increases the **volume** decreases and **rest period** increases.
*As the **load** decreases the **volume** increases and **rest period** decreases.

Training intensity: An individual's level of effort compared with his or her maximal effort; usually expressed as a percentage.

Rest period: The time taken between sets or exercises to rest or recover.

Rest Period and Percent Recovery		Rest Period by Phase	
Amount of Rest	*Percent Recovery*	*Phase of OPT Model*	*Rest Period*
20 - 30 seconds	50%	Stabilization Endurance	0 - 90 seconds
40 seconds	75%	Strength Endurance and Hypertrophy	0 - 60 seconds
60 seconds	85% - 90%	Maximal Strength	3 - 5 minutes
3 - 5 minutes	100%	Power	3 - 5 minutes

Exercise selection: The process of choosing exercises that allow for achievement of the desired adaptation. *Exercises should be specific to the client's desired training goals.*

Multi-joint exercise: Involves two or more muscle groups & joints during the exercise. *(Deadlifts, squats & bench press are examples of multi-joint exercises)*

Single-joint exercise: Isolated muscle group exercises involving one joint movement. *(Bicep curls, knee extensions & leg curls are some examples of single-joint exercises)*

Unilateral: Exercises or movements involving one limb. *(One arm bicep curl is an example)*

Bilateral: Exercises or movements involving both limbs. *(Barbell bench press is an example)*

Push exercises: Exercises involving the *"push"* muscle groups. *(Bench press, squat & abduction)*

Pull exercises: Exercises involving the *"pull"* muscle groups. *(Pull-ups, deadlifts & adduction)*

In addition to client's goals, there are also important lifestyle factors to take into consideration when designing their program. How much stress they encounter daily, how much sleep they get, and how well they eat can influence program design.

The **order of exercises** should be prioritized according to the **client's needs and goals**. Greater strength gains are seen in the exercises that are performed first due to the greater number of reps and sets *(volume)* one can perform when they are fresh. Ideally, an exercise session should start with the largest muscle group or most complex exercise and progress to smaller muscle groups and less complex movements. The following are general recommendations when deciding the order of exercises:

- Large muscle groups before small muscle groups
- Multi-joint before single-joint exercises
- Alternate push/pull exercises for total body sessions
- Alternate upper/lower body exercises for total body sessions
- Explosive/power type lifts & plyometric exercises before basic strength and single-joint
- Exercises for priority weak areas before exercises for strong areas
- Most intense to least intense

10 common strengthening exercises that are effective for most individuals:

1) Supine floor bridge
2) Prone Iso-abs (Plank)
3) Scaption (functional shoulder exercise)
4) Single-leg balance reach
5) Squat jump to stabilization
6) Back row
7) Squat to row
8) Squat
9) Lunge
10) Deadlift

The OPT Model: Optimum Performance Training

The OPT Model (Optimum Performance Training)		
Phase 1	Stabilization Endurance	Stabilization
Phase 2	Strength Endurance	Strength
Phase 3	Hypertrophy	
Phase 4	Maximal Strength	
Phase 5	Power	Power

Typically a phase of training last 4 weeks as this is the general timeframe for the body to adapt to a given stimulus.

Physiological benefits:

- Improved cardiorespiratory efficiency
- Enhanced beneficial endocrine *(hormone)* and serum lipid *(cholesterol)* adaptations
- Increased metabolic efficiency *(metabolism)*
- Increased tissue tensile strength *(tendons, ligaments, muscles)*
- Increased bone density

Physical benefits:

- Decreased body fat
- Increased lean muscle mass

Performance benefits:

- Improved flexibility
- Better balance
- Enhanced endurance
- Improved speed, agility, and quickness
- Greater strength
- More power

Integrated Fitness Training is a comprehensive training approach that combines all the components necessary to help a client achieve optimum performance. Includes all of the following elements of effective movement: ***Flexibility, Cardiorespiratory, Core, Balance, Reactive, Speed, Agility, Quickness (SAQ), and Resistance training.***

The progressions within the OPT model are divided up to support each component of integrated fitness training mentioned above and each level ***(Stabilization, Strength, and Power).***

The Optimum Performance Training (OPT) Model: Applying Stabilization

The stabilization level of the OPT model is the foundation for all subsequent training phases that follow. The following list the goals of Stabilization Endurance *(Phase 1)* training:

- Increase stability
- Increase muscular endurance
- Increase control in all planes of motion
- Increase coordination of movement

Stabilization: The human movement system's ability to provide optimal dynamic joint support to maintain correct posture during all movements.

Proprioception: The ability to recognize bodily movement and position.

Time under tension (TUT): The amount of time from the beginning of one resistance training set to the end without breaking.

Timed hold: An acute variable where the requirement is to hold a specific pose or posture for a specified period of time. *Time holds can include the pallof press hold, prone iso-abs, single-leg balance, and squat jump to stabilization (reps and timed holds combined).*

Horizontal loading: Performing all sets of an exercise or body part before moving on to the next exercise or body part.

Vertical loading: Circuit applied to more conditioned clients allowing alternating body parts to be trained from set to set, starting from the upper extremity and moving to the lower extremity with little to no rest in between.

Intensity levels in the stabilization phase are dictated by the amount of instability or proprioception that is added or removed.

Movement preparation is the systematic implementation of flexibility, core, balance, reactive, and SAQ *(when applicable)* training principles prior to completing the remaining majority portion of the workout *(usually resistance portion)*. *Movement prep prepares the body for the work that follows.*

The **stabilization phase** is performed with **controlled tempos** and **high repetitions** which increases the time under tension (TUT). All of the following acute variables dictate the overall volume of training:

Stabilization (Phase 1) Acute Variables							
	Reps	Sets	Tempo	Interval	Frequency	Duration	Exercise Selection
Flexibility	1	1 - 3	30-second hold	N/A	3 - 7 times/week	4 - 6 weeks	SMR and static
Core	12 - 20	1 - 4	4/2/1	0 - 90 seconds	2 - 4 times/week	4 - 6 weeks	1 - 4 core stabilization
Balance	12 - 20 or 6 - 10 each side for single leg	1 - 3	4/2/1 if applicable 0-60 second timed holds if tempo is not applicable	0 - 90 seconds	2 - 4 times/week	4 - 6 weeks	1 - 4 balance stabilization
Plyometric	5 - 8	1 - 3	3 – 5 second hold on landing	0 - 90 seconds	2 - 4 times/week	4 - 6 weeks	0 - 2 plyometric stabilization
SAQ	2 - 3	1 - 2	Controlled for effective movement patterns	0 - 90 seconds	2 - 4 times/week	4 - 6 weeks	4 - 6 drills with limited horizontal inertia and unpredictability
Resistance	12 - 20	1 - 3	4/2/1	0 - 90 seconds	2 - 4 times/week	4 - 6 weeks	1 - 2 stabilization progression

Tempo is listed in seconds as *(eccentric contraction / isometric hold / concentric contraction)*.
12 reps is equivalent to **75% intensity**
20 reps is equivalent to **50% intensity**

SMR & Flexibility Protocols in the Stabilization Level

Davis's Law states that soft tissue will align along the lines of stress that are placed upon it.

Phase 1 of the stabilization level consists of **corrective flexibility** which requires a combination of **self-myofascial release (SMR)** and **static stretching**.

When performing SMR, gentle pressure should be applied to the trigger point *(tight area)* for a minimum of 30 seconds to allow for autogenic inhibition and a relaxation response. *When foam-rolling one should hold the position on this trigger area for a minimum of 30 seconds rather than rolling back and forth.*

Contracting the antagonist *(opposing muscles)* when performing static stretches allows the muscle being stretched to further relax and enhance the stretch. *, e.g., A person can contract (squeeze) their gluteus maximus when performing a kneeling hip flexor stretch to **reciprocally inhibit** the hip flexors allowing additional lengthening of the hip flexors.*

Core Protocols in the Stabilization Level

The core is defined as the LPHC, thoracic and cervical spine. An increase in muscular endurance and stabilization of the core while performing movements is the goal of training in phase 1.

Proximal stability promotes **Distal** mobility *When the core is stable and strong distal movements involving the arms & legs can be performed more efficiently.*

When identifying compensations that warrant corrective core stabilization exercises the fitness professional should pay attention to which plane of motion the compensation takes place. Once identified appropriate corrective exercises can be implemented. Below are some examples of compensations and their associated planes:

- *Anterior pelvic tilt (low back arches)*: Sagittal plane compensation
- *Hip shift*: Frontal/transverse plane compensation
- *Hip rotation*: Transverse plane compensation

Balance Protocols in the Stabilization Level

Center of gravity (COG): The area within an object at which the weight is equally balanced in all directions. In a person, this is generally around the navel but can change depending on the posture/movement of the body.

Base of Support (BOS): The area beneath an object or person that includes every point of contact that the object or person makes with the supporting surface. In people these points of contact are usually the feet or hands.

Balance is the ability to maintain the body's center of gravity (COG) over its base of support (BOS). The goal of balance training is to keep the center of gravity (COG) over the base of support (BOS).

The following are examples of balance stabilization exercises: *Single-leg balance, Single-leg lift & chop, Single-leg hip internal and external rotation.*

Reactive Protocols in the Stabilization Level

Reactive stabilization focuses on landing mechanics. The goal in this phase is to develop good movement patterns and landing motions so that the client can avoid injury.

Reactive training performed in Phase 1 *(Stabilization)* of the OPT Model focuses on static 3 – 5 second holds in the landing positions whereas **Plyometric training** is a type of reactive training performed in Phase 5 *(Power)* level of the OPT Model.

SAQ Protocols in the Stabilization Level

Speed, Agility, and Quickness (SAQ) training is optional in the stabilization level depending on the client's goals. The goal is to develop a base level of agility and quickness so the client can move functionally at applicable speeds in a dynamic *(moving/changing)* environment. Clients must demonstrate sufficient core and balance stabilization prior to engaging in SAQ drills.

Cardiorespiratory Training Protocols in the Stabilization Level

The **SAID principle** *(Specific Adaptations to Imposed Demands)* applies to cardiorespiratory training as well. The cardiorespiratory system adapts based on the stimulus it is given. Varying the type of cardiorespiratory training will continue to elicit stress which causes adaptation while also reducing the risk of overtraining.

Clients who have muscle imbalances should perform corrective flexibility programs *prior* to completing their cardio sessions during the stabilization level. Performing cardio without proper flexibility can make compensations and muscle imbalances worse.

A 5-10 minute warm-up is recommended before each cardio training session.

The **goal of Phase 1** of cardiorespiratory training is to **build the clients aerobic base**. This will lay the foundation for more intense methods of training in the later phases. The client is ready to move to the next phase of the OPT model once they can successfully **complete 30 minutes of steady state cardio (without stopping) at 65%-70% of their max heart rate (HR_{max}).**

FITTE Principle: Frequency, Intensity, Time, Type, and Enjoyment

FITTE Principle applied to Cardiorespiratory Training (Phase 1)	
F *(Frequency)*	3 – 5 days per week
I *(Intensity)*	65%-75% HR_{max}, 12-13 on RPE scale, or ability to maintain a conversation with talk test.
T *(Time)*	30 – 60 minutes
T *(Type)*	Exercises that are rhythmic, use large muscle groups, and/or are continuous in nature
E *(Enjoyment)*	Do what you *like* to do, not necessarily what you think you *should* do. Always keep enjoyment of exercise in mind!

Common Mistakes Made in the Stabilization Level

- Underutilized assessments
- Lack of protocol, programming, or formulated means of progression
- Desire to progress too soon
- Focusing on stabilization or endurance, but not both

The Optimum Performance Training (OPT) Model: Applying Strength

The strength level of the OPT model consists of the following (3) Phases: *Strength Endurance (Phase 2), Hypertrophy (Phase 3), and Maximal Strength (Phase 4).* The goal is to develop strength to promote optimal performance of the body.

- Increase the core muscles ability to stabilize the lumbo-pelvic hip complex (LPHC) and spine during heavier loads and through complex ranges of motion *(strength endurance).*
- Improve metabolic conditioning.
- Increase the load-bearing capabilities of muscles, tendons, ligaments, and joints *(strength endurance and hypertrophy).*
- Increase the volume of training to stimulate muscle tissue growth *(hypertrophy).*
- Increase motor unit recruitment, frequency of motor unit activation, and motor unit synchronization *(maximal strength).*

Metabolic conditioning: Exercise that improves effective and efficient energy storage and delivery of physical activity.

Exercise tolerance: Increased ability to perform more exercise in less time, without undue fatigue or excessive soreness.

Motor unit activation: Increased recruitment of motor units and/or recruitment of motor units rapidly and repeatedly.

Neural drive: The frequency of activation signals sent to muscle fibers via motor neurons.

Muscle coordination: Complex neurological control of motor units, ensuring effective contraction and relaxation of muscle tissue across agonists and antagonist muscle groups.

Strength endurance: The ability of the body to repeatedly produce high levels of force for prolonged periods.

Diminishing returns: As the systems of the body become more developed, the rate of improvement in fitness slows.

Muscular failure: A training approach that involves the completion of as many reps as possible until the individual is unable to complete a repetition due to fatigue.

Maintenance: Sustaining developed levels of muscular fitness without improvement.

*Strength training will not produce large amounts of muscle growth in women due to the lower androgen levels that women have compared to men.

SMR & Flexibility Protocols in the Strength Level

Self-Myofascial Release (SMR) is useful during the warm-up, movement prep, and cool-down portions of a workout during the strength level of the OPT Model. SMR can help to improve range of motion (ROM) and muscular performance.

Active-isolated stretching should also be used during the strength level. Active-isolated stretching allows for agonist and synergists muscles to move a limb through a full range of motion (ROM) while the antagonists are being stretched.

Core Protocols in the Strength Level

The goal of core training in the strength level is to strengthen the deep and superficial muscles that stabilize, align, and move the trunk of the body.

Balance Protocols in the Strength Level

Balance training in the strength level contributes to the safety and effectiveness of resistance training for strength adaptations. In this level, balance training should incorporate dynamic eccentric and concentric movements through a full range of motion (ROM). The following are examples of balance strength exercises:

- Single-leg squat
- Single-leg squat touchdown
- Single-leg Romanian deadlift
- Single-leg Lift and Chop
- Multiplanar lunge to balance

Reactive Training Protocols in the Strength Level

Reactive training in the strength level should progress from stabilization level involving more dynamic eccentric and concentric movement through a full range of motion (ROM). Below are some examples of reactive strength exercises:

- Tuck jump
- Butt kick
- Jumping lunges

SAQ Protocols in the Strength Level

SAQ training in the strength level can help improve sports performance and function of activities of daily living *(helps fall prevention due to increased spatial awareness and proprioception)*. SAQ drills in this level can include the following:

- Agility ladder drills
- Cone drills
- Hurdle drills
- Reaction drills

Strength Level Acute Variables (Phases 2, 3 & 4)							
	Reps	Sets	Tempo	Rest	Frequency	Duration	Exercise Selection
Flexibility (SMR)	1	1 - 2	Minimum of 30-second holds	N/A	3 - 7 days/week	4 weeks	SMR
Flexibility (Active-isolated Stretching)	5 - 10	1 - 2	1 - 2 second holds	N/A	3 - 7 days/week	4 weeks	Active-isolated
Core	8 - 12	2 - 3	Medium 2/0/2 Use 1/1/1 for Max Strength	0 - 60 seconds	2 - 4 days/week	4 weeks	* 1 - 3 core strength endurance * 0 - 4 for Hypertrophy * 0 - 3 for Max Strength
Balance	8 - 12	2 - 3	Medium 2/0/2 Use 1/1/1 for Max Strength	0 - 60 seconds	2 - 4 days/week	4 weeks	* 1 - 3 balance strength endurance * 0 - 4 for Hypertrophy * 0 - 3 for Max Strength
Plyometric	8 - 10	2 - 3	Repeating	0 - 60 seconds	2 - 4 days/week	4 weeks	* 1 - 3 plyometric strength endurance * 0 - 4 for Hypertrophy * 0 - 3 for Max Strength
SAQ	3 – 5	3 - 4	Fast	0 - 60 seconds	2 - 4 days/week	4 weeks	6 - 8 drills allowing greater horizontal inertia but limited unpredictability

Resistance Training Protocols in the Strength Level

Progressive Resistance Exercise (PRE): A method of increasing the ability of muscles to generate force.

Benefits of resistance training for both men & women include the following:

- Increased strength
- Improved quality of life
- Increase or maintenance of bone mineral density
- Decreased risk of falls during activities of daily living
- Decreased risk of injury during sport activities
- Improved blood cholesterol
- Increased metabolic rate *(calories burned at rest)*

Strength Level Acute Variables (Phases 2, 3 & 4) for Resistance Training								
	Reps	Sets	Tempo	Intensity	Rest	Frequency	Duration	Exercise Selection
Phase 2: Strength Endurance	8 - 12	2 - 4	Strength 2/0/2 Stabilization 4/2/1	70 - 80%	0 - 60 seconds	2 - 4 times/week	4 weeks	1 Strength superset w/ 1 Stabilization
Phase 3: Hypertrophy	6 - 12	3 - 5	2/0/2	75 - 85%	0 - 60 seconds	3 - 6 times/week	4 weeks	2-4 Strength exercises / body part
Phase 4: Maximal Strength	1 - 5	4 - 6	X/X/X	85 - 100%	3-5 min	2 - 4 times/week	4 weeks	1-3 Strength exercises

Cardiorespiratory Training Protocols in the Strength Level

It is important to continue cardiorespiratory training in the strength level of the OPT Model. The focus of cardio training in this level is to increase the workload in a way that will help clients alter their heart rate in and out of Zones 1 and 2. This stage introduces interval training gradually under the guidelines of the *General Adaptation Syndrome (GAS)*.

*High-Intensity Interval Training (HIIT) is not performed in this stage.

Concurrent training: Training designed to maintain or improve multiple fitness components in the same training phase.

When prescribing both cardiorespiratory and resistance training in the same session the goals of the client should dictate the order of exercise. For example, someone seeking hypertrophy would perform resistance training first while someone looking to increase endurance would perform cardio first.

Common Mistakes Made in the Strength Level

- Failure to adjust training variables based on individual training status.
- Utilizing the same group of exercises for all clients regardless of their individual needs.
- Failure to alter training in a coordinated fashion over time.
- Prescribing training to muscular failure for lengthy periods of time.
- Creating excessive muscle soreness by overprescribing intense training.

Proper form is essential and should be corrected as necessary during any exercise that is performed.

Movement assessments should be performed every 30 days *(4 weeks)*. Corrective exercise strategies should be adjusted as necessary based on the findings of assessments. Corrective exercises can be incorporated into the warm-up, movement prep & as a superset with a strength exercise.

The Optimum Performance Training (OPT) Model: Applying Power

The primary goal in the **power level** of the OPT Model is to increase the rate of force production *(muscle contraction)* within the kinetic chain. This increase allows clients to better perform activities of daily living and sports while also decreasing the risk of injury. Increasing the rate of **force production** is accomplished by enhancing **neuromuscular efficiency** and **prime mover strength**.

Power = Force x Velocity

The **power level** consists of **low volume, high intensity,** and **ample rest** between sessions.

In order to progress to the power level of the OPT Model one must possess core and joint stability, a good strength base, optimal range of motion (ROM) around key joints such as the hips and ankles, and good neuromuscular control.

Benefits of the power level include the following:

- Increase muscular power and strength
- Improve bone health
- Reduce the effects of aging
- Improve sports performance

Force-Velocity Curve shows that peak power is best achieved around 60-70% of maximal force and 30-40% of maximal velocity.

Proprioceptors: Sensors in muscles and tendons that provide information about joint angle, muscle length, and muscle tension. *(Muscle spindles, Golgi Tendon Organs (GTOs)*

Sarcopenia: The loss of muscle tissue as a natural result of the aging process.

Anaerobic power: Maximum power *(work per unit time)* that is the result of all-out, high-intensity physical output without the use of oxygen. It is a reflection of the short-term effects of the intramuscular high-energy phosphates – adenosine triphosphates (ATP) and phosphocreatine (PCr).

Anterior cruciate ligament (ACL): One of the four ligaments in the knee that connects the femur to the tibia.

Most sports injuries occur during deceleration. Therefore training eccentric strength will help improve one's ability to decelerate and minimize injury risk.

Henneman's size principle: Motor units which are under load are recruited from smallest to largest.

The acute variables to stimulate type II *(fast-twitch)* muscle fibers are as follows: *Greater than or equal to 85% of 1RM, six or fewer reps, sets, and 2-5 minute rest periods.*

Metabolic conditioning circuit: A high-intensity exercise circuit designed to increase the storage and delivery of energy for any activity. It primarily conditions the phosphagen and glycolytic pathways.

Training age refers to the number of years a client has been training.

Movement prep in the power level should prime the nervous system for the more rigorous work that follows.

SMR & Flexibility Protocols in the Power Level

Dynamic stretching is utilized during the power level. The following are examples of dynamic stretches that can be used in the power level: *Prisoner squat, multiplanar lunges, single-leg touchdown, tube walking, medicine ball lift and chop.*

Core Protocols in the Power Level

Core exercises in the power level involve trunk movements that are performed as quickly and safely as possible with light resistance. *(rotation chest pass, medicine ball throw, soccer throw)*

Balance Protocols in the Power Level

Balance training in the power level involves dynamic movements performed in a controlled manner.

Reactive Protocols in the Power Level

Reactive exercises are the required exercises for training in the power level. They can be performed as part of the movement prep, combined in a superset with resistance training, or performed on off-days as their own workout. Faster reaction times contribute to an increase in speed and power.

SAQ Protocols in the Power Level

Common SAQ exercises for the power level include the following:

- Partner mirror drill
- Agility ball drill
- Star cone drill
- Dynamic ladder drills

Power Level Acute Variables (Phases 5)							
	Reps	Sets	Tempo	Rest	Frequency	Duration	Exercise Selection
Flexibility (SMR)	1	0 - 2	Minimum of 30-second holds	N/A	3-7 days/week	4 weeks	SMR
Flexibility (Dynamic Stretches)	10 - 15	1 - 2	Controlled	N/A	3-7 days/week	4 weeks	3 - 10 dynamic exercises
Core	8 - 12	2 - 3	X/X/X	0 - 60 seconds	2-4 days/week	4 weeks	0 - 2 core power
Balance	8 - 12	2 - 3	Controlled	0 - 60 seconds	2-4 days/week	4 weeks	0 - 2 balance power
Plyometric	8 - 12	2 - 3	X/X/X	0 - 60 seconds	2-4 days/week	4 weeks	0 - 2 plyometric power
SAQ	3 - 5 run throughs	3 - 5	X/X/X	0 - 90 seconds	2-4 days/week	4 weeks	6 - 10 drills allowing maximal horizontal inertia & unpredictability

Resistance Protocols in the Power Level

Superset training is the preferred method used in the power level. Superset training is one exercise immediately followed by another exercise with no rest. Using supersets in the power level train both force and velocity which increase power.

Using a maximal strength exercise *(heavier weight 85%-100% of 1RM)* followed immediately by a similar movement power exercise *(lighter weight 30%-45% of 1RM)* performed at maximal speed trains both of these variables to increase overall power *(e.g., Bench press followed by power push-ups).*

Benefits of power phase supersets *(post-activation potentiation)*:

- Increased neuromuscular stimulation that leads to slow-twitch type 1 fibers behaving more like fast-twitch fibers.

- More direct electrical stimulation *(potentiation)* to the muscle.

- Reflex potentiation (enhanced H-reflex), which increases the efficiency and rate of nerve impulses to the muscles.

- Increased synchronization of motor unit firing.

- Reduced inhibition from the GTOs.

- Enhanced reciprocal inhibition of the antagonist muscles.

- Increased phosphorylation *(for ATP production)* of myosin, during a maximal voluntary contraction *(MVC)*, leading to faster rates of muscular contraction and tension.

Power Level Acute Variables (Phases 5) for Resistance Training							
Reps	Sets	Tempo	Intensity	Rest	Frequency	Duration	Exercise Selection
1 - 5 (Strength) 8 - 10 (Power)	3 - 5	X/X/X (Strength) X/X/X (Power)	85 - 100% (Strength) Up to 10% body weight or 30 - 45% of 1RM (Power)	1 - 2 min between supersets 3 - 5 min between circuits	2 - 4 times/ week	4 weeks	1 Strength superset with 1 Power exercise

Cardiorespiratory Training in the Power Level

Cardio training in the power level should focus on the anaerobic system *(without oxygen)* rather than the slow endurance type aerobic training *(with oxygen)* which can actually hinder power output. The anaerobic system is triggered by *High-Intensity Interval Training (HIIT)*. A 10 minute warm up in Zone 1 is followed by an increase in workload every 60 seconds until the client reaches Zone 3. Once Zone 3 is met alternating intervals between Zones 2 & 3 ideally at a 1:1 ratio is performed for up to 30 minutes. Times should be adjusted based on clients response and ability to reduce heart rate back to Zone 2.

Cardiorespiratory Training Zones	
Zone 1 *(Recovery)*	HR_{max} (65-75%) RPE = 12-13
Zone 2 *(Lactate Threshold)*	HR_{max} (76-85%) RPE = 14-16
Zone 3 *(Peak/Interval)*	HR_{max} (86-95%) RPE = 17-19

*RPE (Ratings of Perceived Exhaustion)

Common Mistakes Made in the Power Level

- Too much volume
- Not using proper regressions
- Inappropriate exercise selection
- Not cueing intensity

The Optimum Performance Training (OPT) Model: Every Day

The OPT Model is designed as a guide that is flexible and can be adjusted when necessary while still meeting the client's needs. The fitness professional should be prepared to adjust a program depending on a client's schedule, equipment availability, injuries, and/or illness.

Modality: A form or mode of exercise that presents a specific stress to the body. Training modalities fall into the following categories:

- Bodyweight training
- Suspension training
- Free weights and implements
- Resistance machines
- Ropes
- Vibration exercise
- Rolling acute resistance

Bodyweight exercise: Form of resistance training where the source of resistance is the weight of the body.

Calisthenics: A form of bodyweight training that uses rhythmic full-body movements.

Suspension training (TRX): The combined use of straps and body weight to place a stress load on the neuromuscular system. *Improves muscular endurance, strength, and stability.*

Free weights: Unrestricted objects of various weights that can be used as resistance for exercise movements. *(Barbells, dumbbells, kettlebells, medicine balls, sandbags, etc.)*

Implement: A unique, free-standing object that can be used as resistance.

Functional movements: Movements based on real-world biomechanics and activities.

Metabolic resistance training: The use of high work-rate resistance activities with few or no recovery intervals.

Dyspnea: Difficulty or troubled breathing.

Heart rate variability: Variations in the time interval between heartbeats. *Indication of fitness*

Extended healthcare providers: Professionals in the healthcare system such as physicians, physical therapists, and cardiac rehabilitation therapists who provide specialized guidance to patients suffering from various physical illnesses or impairments.

Weekend Warriors: Clients who work busy jobs or live sedentary lifestyles during the week but try to maintain participation in moderate to aggressive weekend recreational activities.

Populations with Special Considerations

Special population is a group of people who have similar conditions or characteristics that require alterations to the general exercise plan. Special populations include the following:

Youth: Children and adolescents between the ages of 5 and 18 years.

Limited ability to sweat in hot and humid environments due to immature thermoregulatory systems and lower body mass.

Older adults: Individuals aged 65 years or older.

Prenatal: Individuals who are pregnant.

Postnatal: Individuals who have recently given birth.

Obese: Individuals with a Body Mass Index (BMI) of 30 or above.

Hypertension: Chronically high blood pressure as defined by a systolic pressure above 140 mm Hg and/or diastolic blood pressure above 90 mm Hg.

Coronary heart disease: The coronary arteries of the heart become narrowed due to fatty build up along the walls of the arteries.

Congestive heart failure: A complex condition that is defined by impairment of the heart.

Atherosclerosis: Narrowing of the arteries due to a buildup of plaque along their walls.

Peripheral artery disease: Condition in which blood flow to the extremities is reduced due to narrowing of arteries.

Stroke: Condition in which blood supply to the brain or areas of the brain is greatly reduced or interrupted.

Cancer: Condition in which there is an uncontrollable abnormal growth of cells within the body.

Osteoporosis: Condition in which the bones become fragile and brittle due to reduced bone mass.

All clients must be cleared by their primary care physician before beginning an exercise program. Fitness professionals must understand their scope of practice when working with special populations and refer and communicate with the client's physician regularly. Fitness professionals are not qualified to diagnose or treat medical conditions and should work within the recommended guidelines set by the client's physician.

Special Populations Resistance Training Acute Variables

	Frequency	Volume	Repetitions	Intensity	Rest
Youth	2-3 days/week	1 - 5 sets	3 - 30 per set	45%-85% of 1RM	Varies
Older adults	1-3 days/week	1 - 5 sets	2 - 20 per set	30%-85% of 1RM	Varies
Prenatal	1-3 days/week	1 - 3 sets	12 -20 per set	<70% of 1RM for 1st & 2nd Trimester	2 minutes minimum
Postnatal	2-3 days/week	1 - 3 sets	10 -15 per set	<50% of 1RM	Varies
Obese	1-3 days/week	1 - 4 sets	8 - 15 per set	40%-80% of 1RM	Varies
High blood pressure	Varies	1 set	12 -15 per set	60% of 1RM	Varies
Cardiorespiratory disease	2-3 days/week	2 - 3 sets	8 - 15 per set	40%-80% of 1RM	Varies
Stroke	2-3 days/week	1 - 3 sets	10 -15 per set	40%-80% of 1RM	Varies
Cancer	1-3 days/week	1 - 4 sets	6 -10 per set	50%-80% of 1RM	Varies
Osteoporosis	2-4 days/week	1 - 6 sets	5 - 25 per set	40%-70% of 1RM	Varies

Reactive training for the youth should have 20 - 300 reps per sessions with all other variables remaining the same.

Special Populations Cardiorespiratory Training Acute Variables

	Frequency	Duration	Intensity
Obese	5 days/week	20-60 min per session	40%-80% of HR_{max}
High blood pressure	3-7 days/week	20-60 min per session	40%-85% of HR_{max}
Cardiorespiratory disease	5-7 days/week	20-45 min per session	40%-60% of HR_{max}
Stroke	3-7 days/week	20-60 min per session	50%-80% of HR_{max}
Cancer	1-5 days/week	20-30 min per session	60%-80% of VO_{2max}
Osteoporosis	2-5 days/week	20-60 min per session	60%-90% of HR_{max}

Group Training and the OPT Model

Group training is an exercise setting where one trainer provides tailored exercise guidance to two or more individuals simultaneously.

The size of the group that is being trained should be small enough that the fitness professional can still provide individual attention to each client when necessary.

Corporate fitness: Implementation of health and fitness programming by a fitness professional within a company structure. The following are benefits of a corporate fitness program:

- Medical cost savings for the company. *($2-$4 dollar savings for every $1 spent)*
- Decreased healthcare usage by fitter employees
- Decreased absenteeism
- Increased work productivity
- Increased job satisfaction
- Lower job-related injury rates
- Fewer workers' compensation claims

Emerging **fitness technologies and trends** can aid fitness professionals by helping to improve the health and fitness of their clients. Common fitness technologies include the following: *Smartphone Apps, Activity Trackers, Social Media, and Wearable Technology.*

Wearable Technology: Devices that are worn during exercise and collect/transmit information regarding performance and physiological variables relating to the workout.

Domain 4: Exercise Technique & Training Instruction

The following areas are covered in this domain:

- Integrated Flexibility Training
- Integrated Core Training
- Integrated Reactive Training
- Integrated Balance Training
- Speed, Agility, and Quickness *(SAQ)* Training
- Integrated Resistance Training
- Spotting Techniques
- Cueing
- Types of Learners
- Types of Feedback
- Client Feedback

Integrated Flexibility Training

Flexibility: The normal extensibility of soft tissue, which allows a joint to be moved through its full range of motion.

When flexibility is limited, faulty movement patterns arise and are reinforced during exercise. Flexibility training improves the communication between the nervous system and the muscular system.

Relative flexibility: The human movement system's way of finding the path of least resistance during movement.

Corrective exercise: The programming process that identifies neuromuscular dysfunction, develops a plan of action, and implements a corrective strategy as a part of an exercise training program.

The Flexibility Continuum consists of (3) phases: Corrective, Active, and Functional.

- **Corrective flexibility**: Flexibility training that is applied with the goal of improving muscle imbalances and correcting altered joint mechanics. Self-myofascial release *(foam-rolling)* and *static stretching* are used for corrective flexibility. *Performed in Phase 1 of the OPT Model.*

- **Active flexibility** uses *active-isolated stretching* where the agonist and its synergist muscles move a limb through a full range of motion, allowing the antagonists to stretch.

- **Functional flexibility** uses *dynamic stretching* which requires multiplanar extensibility with optimal neuromuscular control through a full range of motion. Body weight squats, hip swings, multiplanar lunges, and medicine ball lift & chop are examples of dynamic stretching. *Performed in Phase 5 of the OPT Model.*

Self-Myofascial Release (SMR)

Roll slowly on foam roller at 1 inch per second until a tender spot is found. Once found **hold on this spot for 30 seconds** or until the tenderness begins to decrease. This causes Golgi tendon organ (GTO) activity and decreases muscle spindle activity, thus triggering an autogenic inhibitory response. *A tender spot is defined as pain/discomfort classified as 6-9 from a 1-10 point scale. **SMR is used during all phases of the OPT Model***

Performing SMR helps to break up tight areas and knots in the *Fascia*: A strong web of connective tissue that wraps and surrounds muscle fibers, bones, nerves, and blood vessels. The myofascial system covers individual muscles as well as connecting groups of larger muscles together. It provides structural support and protection. *Plural form is **Fasciae**.*

Common SMR form mistakes include the following:

- Rolling too quickly.
- Not identifying the tender spot.
- Not holding static pressure on the tender spot.
  Holding with no movement on tender spot / trigger point helps to release it.
- Tensing the body in the presence of discomfort.
  Relax the muscle and focus on deep breathing.

Static Stretching

Take the stretch to point of tension and **hold for 30-60 seconds**. Static stretches should focus on the overactive *(tight, shortened)* muscles that are identified through assessments. Avoid holding breath & continue to breathe during stretches.

Active-Isolated Stretching

Take the stretch to the first point of tension and **hold for 1-2 seconds**. Repeat this for 5-10 repetitions per set. Active-Isolated stretches should be performed after SMR and static stretches of the same muscles.

Dynamic Stretching

Dynamic stretching should stimulate normal functional movement. These stretches are performed at smooth and controlled speeds for up to 10 reps per set. Dynamic stretching involves moving parts of the body through their full available range of motion.

Passive stretching

Person stretching is not actively involved. The person assumes a position and then either holds it with another part of the body or with assistance from a partner or some other apparatus *(resistance band, towel, etc.)*

Stretching Tips

- Hold stretches for appropriate timeframes *(min 30 seconds)* to allow for the inhibitory response and muscle relaxation caused by Golgi Tendon Organs (GTOs) and muscle spindles.

- Always breathe during stretches and avoid tensing up and holding breath.

- Joints should never be taken past their normal range of motion while performing these various stretching techniques.

Integrated Core Training

The drawing-in maneuver is performed by drawing the navel *(belly button)* back toward the spine without spinal flexion. This maneuver activates the inner core and contracts the transverse abdominus bilaterally to form a corset, which is thought to increase the stability of the lumbar spine. **Performing the "cat" exercise from the quadruped position (all fours) is an example of the drawing-in maneuver.*

Abdominal bracing is the tightening of the outer unit muscles *(rectus abdominus, external obliques, and gluteus maximus)* by consciously contracting them. Performing abdominal bracing causes lumbo-pelvic stiffness which leads to spinal stability. **Prone iso-abs / plank position is an example of abdominal bracing.*

*Note abdominal bracing can increase intra-abdominal pressure if the client holds their breath while bracing *(Valsalva maneuver).* This intra-abdominal pressure can increase the blood pressure and potentially cause the client to pass out. Clients should be reminded to breathe during all exercise.

Integrated Plyometric Training

Plyometric training involves exercises that use quick, powerful movements involving an eccentric contraction immediately followed by an explosive concentric contraction.

*The body will only move within the range of speed that the nervous system has been programmed to allow. Plyometric training works to improve neuromuscular efficiency and the range of speed set by the nervous system.

Plyometric training enhances the following three mechanisms:

- Enhanced muscle spindle activity
- Desensitization of the Golgi tendon organ
- Enhanced neuromuscular efficiency

Rate of force production: Ability of muscles to exert maximal force output in a minimal amount of time.

Motor unit recruitment: The activation of the motor units in a successive manner to produce more strength.

Motor unit synchronization: The simultaneous recruitment of multiple motor units resulting in more muscle tissue contracting at the same time.

Firing frequency: The number of activation signals sent to a single motor unit in 1 second.

Integrated performance paradigm *(stretch-shortening cycle)*: A forceful cycle of muscle contraction that involves eccentric loading of the muscle, isometric muscle contraction *(amortization phase)*, and concentric muscle contraction.

Integrated Balance Training

Balance: Ability to maintain the body's center of gravity within its base of support.

Static balance: Ability to maintain equilibrium in place with no external forces.

Dynamic balance: Ability to maintain equilibrium through the intended path of motion when external forces are present.

Postural stability: Ability to prepare, maintain, anticipate, and restore stability of the entire Human Movement System.

Joint stability: Ability to prepare, maintain, anticipate, and restore stability at each joint.

Perturbation: A disturbance of equilibrium; shaking.

Sensorimotor control: A complex interaction involving the muscular system, PNS, and CNS to obtain balance or postural control.

Sensorimotor integration: The ability of the nervous system to gather and interpret information to anticipate and execute the proper motor response.

Intramuscular coordination is the ability of the neuromuscular system to allow optimal levels of motor unit recruitment and synchronization within a muscle.

Proprioceptively enriched environments are unstable, yet controllable environments used to teach the body how to recruit the right muscle, at the right time, with the right amount of force.

This type of balance training improves force production and injury prevention.

Appropriate balance training progressions are as follows:

- Two-leg stable
- Single-leg stable
- Two-leg unstable
- Single-leg unstable

Speed, Agility, and Quickness (SAQ) Training

SAQ training is beneficial for all individuals, not just athletes. Speed, Agility, and Quickness are valuable attributes that can be used in everyday life. Walking on uneven surfaces, moving out of harm's way, moving to save a falling object or person all require some level of SAQ to perform effectively.

Speed: The straight-ahead velocity of an individual.

Stride rate: The number of strides taken in a given amount of time or distance.

Stride length: The distance covered with each stride.

Agility: The ability to maintain center of gravity over a changing base of support while changing direction at various speeds.

Quickness: The ability to react to a stimulus with an appropriate muscular response without hesitation.

Performing SAQ training correctly with proper form and increasing the speed of performance over time while maintaining proper form is essential when training clients in SAQ.

Integrated Resistance Training

Five major adaptations to resistance training: Stabilization, Endurance, Strength, Hypertrophy, and Power

Strength: Ability of the neuromuscular system to provide internal tension and exert force against external resistance.

Maximal strength: The maximum force a muscle can produce in a single voluntary effort, regardless of the rate of force production.

Power: The ability to produce a large amount of force in a short amount of time. *Power is built upon the foundation of stabilization and strength.*

Resistance Training Systems: Single-Set, Multiple-Set, Pyramid, Superset, Circuit-Training, Peripheral Heart-Action, Tri-Set, and Split-Routine system.

Circuit training is great for those with minimal time who want to change body composition.

Spotting Techniques

Proper spotting techniques reassure the client while performing an exercise and reduce the risk of injury during that exercise. A verbal explanation along with a demonstration of proper lifting technique and form by the fitness professional prior to the client performing the actual exercise will help the client to understand and maintain proper position, form, technique, and control.

Below is a checklist for proper spotting technique:

- Know how many repetitions the lifter intends to do before performing the set.

- Make sure to have a good base of support and are strong enough to assist the lifter with the resistance being used.

- Stop lifters if they break form or have improper technique.

- Provide just enough assistance for the client to successfully complete the lift, helping them through any *"sticking point."*

- Keep hands on or close to the weight being lifted.

- **Spot at the client's forearms near the wrists when using dumbbells, especially for chest press and overhead press exercises.** Certain exercises require spotting with hands on the dumbbell itself such as a dumbbell pullover or overhead dumbbell triceps extension.

Cueing

Cueing is both verbal and nonverbal communication that is used to evoke an action response from participants. Common observations and appropriate cues are listed below:

Observation: A client's knees cave in *(adduct)* during a squat exercise.
Cue: "Keep your knees in line with your second toe."

Observation: A client's lower back begins to arch while performing push-ups.
Cue: "Brace your core" *(abdominal bracing)*

Observation: A client holds their breath while performing static stretches.
Cue: "Continue to breathe slowly to help relax the muscles being stretched."

Types of Learners

Visual: Someone who learns through seeing images & techniques. Visual learners must first see what they are expected to know.

Auditory: A person who learns best through listening. They depend on hearing & speaking as a main way of learning.

Kinesthetic: This learning style requires that you manipulate or touch material to learn. It is often combined with auditory or visual learning techniques producing multi-sensory learning.

"Tell, Show, Do" *Tell me and I'll forget, Show me, and I may remember, Involve me, and I'll understand.* Trainers should keep this proverb in mind when teaching exercises to clients. Using a combination of *"Tell, Show, Do"* is the best practice when teaching. Starting with a brief and simple explanation *"Tell"* along with demonstration *"Show"* followed by the client performing the exercise *"Do*." The personal trainer should observe the client while they perform the exercise and prepare to provide helpful feedback.

Types of Feedback

Evaluative: A summary for the client of how well they have performed a given task.
e.g., "You maintained great form & control during that set."

Supportive: Encourage the client when they perform a task properly. This type of feedback is motivational for the client & helps them adhere to the exercise program.
e.g., "Great job on that last set! Way to finish strong!"

Descriptive: Specific information that helps the client understand what they need to do in order to improve.
e.g., "Make sure to keep your core tight & back straight during the deadlift to protect from injury."

*The type of feedback that provides information on progress can be referred to as ***knowledge of results***.

Client Feedback

Seeking client feedback will help the fitness professional ensure client satisfaction and program enjoyment. Paying attention to both verbal and nonverbal feedback will assist the trainer in properly progressing and modifying the clients training program as needed. Scheduling periodic program evaluations and goal reviews will also ensure client expectations are met.

Domain 5: Client Relations & Behavioral Coaching

The following areas are covered in this domain:

- Building Rapport
- Coaching and Communication Strategies
- Coaching Styles
- The Transtheoretical Model (TTM)
- Goals

Building Rapport

ALF: Always Listen First

APE: Attentive, Peripheral, Empathetic *(types of listening)*

FORM: Family, Occupation, Recreation, and Message *(topic of conversation)*

ALADDER: Ask, Listen, Acknowledge, Dig Deeper, Empathize, Repeat

Rapport is defined as a relationship marked by mutual understanding and trust. This stage begins with the initial first impressions a client has and continues to develop through the use of good verbal and nonverbal communication. A personal trainer should possess excellent communication and teaching skills to create a climate of trust and respect with the client. Look to find common ground with clients so that conversation flows easily. Expressing **empathy**, warmth and genuineness are three attributes to building a successful client-trainer relationship. Anticipating the client's needs shows attention to detail and helps to build rapport. People don't care how much you know until they know how much you care. Future teachings and valuable information that a personal trainer has to share will go unheard if they have not built this foundation of mutual understanding, trust, and respect with their clients. *Positive first impressions are the foundation for the rapport-building process.*

Positive body language:

- Hold a relaxed posture, with a straight back.
- Arms should hang comfortably at the sides. Standing with arms crossed is a sign an individual is closed off to the conversation.
- Maintain eye contact, but avoid staring.
- Speak calmly and confidently

Conversation starters to find common ground and build rapport with potential clients:

- Ask them their name
- Find out where they are from
- Ask where they live now
- Ask about their family
- Ask what they do for a living
- Ask what their hobbies are
- Ask where they see themselves in the future

Earn and keep the trust of clients by expressing the following behaviors: *Dependability, Integrity, and Empathy.*

Maintain credibility by being a *positive role model* who is *honest and consistent.*

Coaching and Communication Strategies

Active Listening: Involves nodding, making eye contact and restating important information the client has stated. Be nonjudgmental and open-minded. Give verbal and nonverbal feedback to indicate attention and understanding. Make sure to receive affirmation from the client on feedback given. Identify statements that indicate a teaching and/or learning opportunity.

Empathize: Match the client's emotions to show affective empathy. The ability to identify with their perspective demonstrates an understanding that helps to develop trust & rapport. *"Seek first to understand, and then to be understood."* – Stephen Covey

Positive Affirmation: Positive words promote positive attitudes & positive outcomes. Positive reinforcement & encouragement help the client to build self-esteem & motivation for exercise.

Intrinsic Motivation: Participation in exercise to achieve internal outcomes such as enjoyment of exercise itself or the sense of accomplishment after the workout is completed. Intrinsic motivation for exercise is better for lifelong adherence to exercise.

Extrinsic Motivation: Participation in exercise to achieve external outcomes such as weight loss & appearance. Extrinsic motivation is good for short-term SMALL goals. External motivation from the fitness professional should inspire intrinsic motivation of the client.

Motivational Interviewing: A collaborative person-centered form of guiding a client to elicit and strengthen motivation for change. The fitness professional should combine empathetic counseling and help the client realize the gap between their values/desires and the unhealthy behavior that is preventing achievement of those goals. Ask open-ended questions that require more than a *"yes"* or *"no"* answer. Encourage the client to talk about what needs to be changed & then help them find ways to elicit that behavior change. Fitness professionals should empower their clients to take control, be independent and self-sufficient with their exercise program by teaching and helping them find enjoyment in the experience. Helping clients take ownership and control increases their intrinsic motivation. A fitness professional should never try to control or manipulate a client into acting a certain way as this will diminish the intrinsic motivation of the client.

Verbal Communication Tips

- Be direct
- Be clear and consistent
- Own your message
- Deliver the messages immediately
- Be supportive
- Be consistent with nonverbal messages *(body language should match verbal message)*
- Look for feedback that the message was actually received and understood.

Characteristics of Professionalism

- Always be at least 5 minutes early.
- Wear appropriate and professional attire.
- Never lose sight of the goal
- Maintain focus on the client.
- Seek to inspire others.

Barriers to Establishing Rapport

- *Not being an active listener.* Active listening involves nodding, making eye contact & restating important information the client has stated.

- *Interrupting too often.* Listen more than you speak, let the client finish their thoughts before acknowledging what they have said or offering input.

- *Being disinterested.* Be in the moment with no distractions, giving 100% of your attention during each interaction with clients.

Coaching Styles

Autonomy-supportive style: A coaching style that focuses on creating an environment that emphasizes self-improvement, rather than competing against others.

Behavior change strategies include the following

- Behavior modification approaches
- Cognitive-behavioral approaches
- Social support approaches
- Self-monitoring
- Cognitive restructuring
- Coping strategies
- Intrinsic approaches.

Behavior modification approaches

- **Prompting**: Promoting an action through encouragement, persuasion, or reminding. *A cue that initiates a behavior.*

- **Contracting**: Agreements between two or more parties that specify expectation, responsibilities, and contingencies for behavior change.

- **Charting attendance and participation**

- **Providing positive feedback on client progress**

Cognitive-Behavioral Approaches

Strategies that address the thoughts and behaviors that provide barriers to fitness to help the client reach their goals.

Association: Focus on internal body feedback *(how muscles or breathing feels)*.

Dissociation: Focus on the external environment *(noticing the scenery or listening to music)*.

Self-monitoring: Ability to recognize and regulate one's behavior.

Cognitive restructuring: Psychotherapeutic process of learning to identify and dispute irrational or maladaptive thoughts.

Cognitive distortions: The mind's way of convincing itself that something true is actually untrue to reinforce negative thinking or emotions.
Eliminate negative self-talk

Coping: Process of managing specific internal or external demands that tax or exceed one's resources.

Problem-focused coping: Targets an issue causing stress to reduce the effects of the stress.

Emotion-focused coping: Distracts from negative feelings associated with stress.

Intrinsic approach: An inside-out approach to exercise that emphasizes the enjoyment and fun of exercise and making it something to look forward to, not just a means to a goal accomplishment. *The best and most long-lasting motivation comes from within.*

The Transtheoretical Model (TTM)

The TTM states that individual's progress through a series of stages of behavior change and that movement through these stages is cyclical *(cycles)*, not linear because any do not succeed in their efforts at establishing and maintaining lifestyle changes.

The TTM Model is composed of these four components: Stages of change, Processes of change, Self-efficacy, and Decisional balance.

Stages of change: Pre-contemplation, Contemplation, Preparation, Action, Maintenance, and Termination. *Know how to determine what stage of change the client is in based on their responses during motivational interviewing.*

Process of change involves using interventions specific to a client's current stage of change to help them transition to the next stage of change. This will help increase the success of the client adopting a new behavior.

Self-Efficacy: The belief in one's own capabilities to successfully engage in a physical-activity program along with one's ability for self-management, goal achievement & effectiveness.

Self-Efficacy *(self-confidence)* is developed through the following sources: Performance accomplishments, Modeling *(vicarious experience)*, Verbal persuasion, and Imaginal experiences *(visualization)*. *Fitness professionals should work to build their clients confidence by using the sources above.*

Trait: A part of an individual's behavior that shapes his or her personality.

State: A temporary change in one's personality, such as an emotion.
The TTM seeks to change the states of an individual, not their traits.

Positive reinforcement: The practice of offering a reward following a desired behavior to encourage repetition of the behavior.
Nonverbal positive reinforcement could be a pat on the back or a smile.
Verbal positive reinforcement could entail saying "Great job today!" or "Way to finish strong!"

Journaling: A type of self-monitoring and a practical way to collect information about behavior patterns that can be used to identify cues and barriers to exercise and nutrition plans.

Influences of Human Behavior include the following:

- Cognitive influences *(self-confidence, self-talk)*
- Affective influences *(positive and negative emotions)*
- Interpersonal influences *(group activities, social support)*
- Behavior influences *(positive reinforcement, self-monitoring)*
- Sensation influences *(pain associated with exercise, feelings of hunger)*

Goals

Objective goal: Something an individual is trying to accomplish; the object or aim of an action.

Subjective goal: Goal based on experience or expectations; less tangible than an objective goal.

Outcome goal: A goal that is usually about winning or losing; in an exercise setting, it is the end result of some behavior. *Winning a weight loss challenge at work.*

Performance goal: A goal that specifies the end products of performance expressed in terms of personal achievement. *Run a 5k in 25 minutes.*

Process goal: A goal that specifies the processes and individual wants to perform in a satisfactory manner. *Eat 2,000 calories per day or exercise 3 times per week.*
Process and performance goals are within the clients control and can be used to achieve outcome goals. It is best to focus on the process instead of the outcome to achieve goals.

Short-term goal: A goal that is set to be achieved within the near future. *Should be process-oriented and work towards achieving a long-term outcome goal.*

Long-term goal: A large goal that is set to be achieved over a long period of time. *Usually made up of a series of smaller short-term goals.*

SMART goals: Specific, Measurable, Attainable, Realistic, Timely *(Time-Bound)*

The following four mechanisms play a role in goal-related behavior change:

- Goals direct attention toward desired behaviors
- Goals lead to greater effort
- Goals extend the time & energy devoted to a desired behavior
- Goals increase the use of goal-relevant skills

Goal commitment is increased when a client is involved in the goal setting process *(when they make their own goals)* or embrace the goals that the fitness professional has helped them create.

"Without involvement, there is no commitment." — Stephen Covey

Progress Evaluation: Evaluating client's progress and providing feedback enhances their motivation and accountability towards achieving the goals set.

Domain 6: Professional Development & Responsibility

The following areas are covered in this domain:

- NASM CPT Scope of Practice
- Continuing Education
- Navigate the Professional Fitness Environment
- Sales & Marketing

NASM Certified Personal Trainer (CPT) Scope of Practice

- Health and fitness professionals who perform individualized assessments and design safe, effective, and individualized exercise and conditioning programs that are scientifically valid and based on clinical evidence to clients with no medical or special needs.

- Provide guidance to help clients achieve their personal health, fitness and performance goals via the implementation of exercise programs, nutritional recommendations, and suggestions in lifestyle modification.

- Hold a current emergency cardiopulmonary resuscitation (CPR) and automated external defibrillator (AED) certification and respond appropriately in emergency situations.

- Do not diagnose and/or treat areas of pain or disease and will refer clients to other healthcare professionals/practitioners, when appropriate.

- Abide by NASM's code of professional conduct at all times.

Know the scope of practice for NASM CPT as well as other adjacent professions such as physicians, athletic trainer, physical therapist, registered dietician so that you know who to refer clients to when necessary.

Continuing education: Any of a variety of course offerings that serve the purpose of keeping professionals up-to-date with their knowledge and skills.

Continuing education unit (CEU): A measure used in continuing education courses that are designed for professionals to maintain a certification or licensure. *NASM CPT's need to obtain 2 CEUs (20 contact hours) of continuing education every 2 years to maintain their certification.*

Best practices: Professional procedures that are considered to be correct, safe, or most effective.

Special population: Individuals who will require modifications or specialized training.

Navigate the Professional Fitness Environment

Demographics: Statistical data relating to the population and the particular groups in it.

Psychographics: The study of personality, values, opinions, attitudes, interests, and lifestyles.

Operations: Activities involved in the day-to-day functions of a business that do not directly generate revenue.

Large-Scale Fitness Facilities: Large budget, high focus on sales, proprietary company systems.

- Front Desk and Operations
- Management
- Maintenance
- Sales Department
- Fitness Department
- Sports and Aquatics
- Child Care and Additional Services

Medium Sized Fitness Facilities: Less densely populated location, less complex membership.

- Front Desk and Operations
- Management
- Fitness Department

Small Group Training Facilities: Community involvement, Shared operational responsibility.

- Sales and Operations
- Management
- Fitness Department

Boutique and High-End Facilities:

- Luxury fitness experience
- Exceptional customer service
- Exclusivity and privacy

Independent Fitness Professionals: Offers the most freedom but also the most responsibility.

Top-line: A company's overall sales or revenues before any discounts or returns.

Driver of sales: Activities that create opportunities for future sales.

Ancillary revenue: Revenue beyond the sale of memberships and services generated by the direct sale of products to customers.

Sales and Marketing

To have a successful career as a fitness professional, you must maintain and be knowledgeable of: *Sales, Service, and Science*

Fitness professionals should have a solid understanding of sales and marketing in order to gain & maintain the necessary number of clients to support their career and achieve desired income.

Leads: Individuals who have shown a certain level of interest in personal training services.

Prospecting: Activities designed to search for potential customers or clients.

Rapport: The aspect of a relationship characterized by similarity, agreement, or congruity.

Point-of-sale client: A client who has purchased a personal training package or program at the time that he or she enrolled in a membership program.

New business: A new client who has purchased personal training services as a result of the fitness professional's prospecting activities.

Re-sign: An existing client who has elected to continue training and purchases additional personal training services or commits contractually to training for a longer period of time.

Forecasting: Process whereby trainers and/or managers apply specific percentages based on previous performance to predict future sales or other measurable outcomes, such as sessions serviced.

Professional networking is an important factor for long-term success in the industry.

Cross-departmental interaction and promotion within the fitness professional's place of work will assist with attaining new clients by way of referral from other departments. Building rapport with employees in other departments is key in establishing effective cross-promotion. The ability to understand other departments and employees *(how they work, what are their motivations, and assist in their efforts)* shows an understanding that helps to develop trust & rapport. *"Seek first to understand, and then to be understood."* – Stephen Covey

Former prospects and follow-ups: Fitness professionals should find out what the prospects preferred way of communicating is *(e-mail, phone, social media, texting)* and follow up with them for notifications and promotions.

The four Ps of Marketing: Product, Price, Placement, and Promotion

Open-ended question: A question that cannot be answered with a simple *"yes"* or *"no*." It gives the person answering the scope to provide more detailed information. Examples listed below.

Why do you want to begin working out?

What are your fitness and health goals?

Complementary goods and services: Goods and services that are similar and share a beneficial relationship with another product or service offering, but are not viewed by the consumer as an alternative or direct competition.

Fitness professionals should create and establish a network of businesses that offer complementary goods and services such as the following:

- Massage therapists
- Supplement and nutrition product distributors
- Sports programs and coaches
- Allied health professionals *(occupational therapists, physical therapists, physicians)*
- Small group training facilities
- Healthy restaurants or grocery stores
- Other outlets that promote healthy lifestyles and activities

Steps to follow when starting with a new prospect client:

- Identify the client's most important fitness goals.
- Complete subjective & various objective assessments.
- Discuss the findings from the assessments.
- Establish a realistic time frame in which fitness goals can be obtained using the phases of the OPT model.

Establishing the framework for an exercise program based on initial assessments and client goals lessens the fitness professionals need to sell to the client. It puts the fitness professional into an educational role where they can help the potential client select the best options *(number of sessions, frequency, etc.)* to meet their goals.

Time & Money are the two most common objections for people when trying to decide on a fitness program. Fitness professionals can use the following four steps to help clients overcome objections:

1) *Validate* the objection to show understanding.
2) *Isolate* focusing solely on the objection presented.
3) *Remind* the person of their WHY, the main reason they searched for a fitness program to refocus them on the importance of reaching their goals.
4) *Resolve* showing the person that there is a plan to achieve their goals will help them believe that it can be accomplished and that the commitment of time, effort, and money will be worth it.

Potential internal barriers to successfully presenting a sale:

- *Fear of rejection.* A failure to convert a sale should not be taken personally. Remember that *"failure is feedback"* so that you can learn and adjust your strategy moving forward.

- *Not working to overcome a prospect's objection.* Always be prepared to *Validate, Isolate, Remind, and Resolve* and objection.

- *Not knowing when to present personal training options to a prospect.* You lose every sale that you do not ask for. Find opportunities to present personal training options through conversations with prospective clients. If they discuss goals, need help with an exercise, or ask a fitness-related question.

- *Not demonstrating enough value to the prospect.* Always seek to over deliver on value. Once you find out the prospects *"why"* you should demonstrate how the exercise program you will design will help them achieve what they desire. Demonstrate your education and credentials *(NASM CPT)* Your ability to hold clients accountable and your ability to motivate.

Conversions

Fat = 9 calories per gram

Protein = 4 calories per gram

Carbohydrates = 4 calories per gram

Alcohol = 7 calories per gram

3500 kcal (calories) = 1 pound of fat

1 Kg = 2.2 pounds *(pounds ÷ 2.2 = Kg)*

1 MET = 3.5 ml *(VO$_2$ ÷ 3.5 = MET)*

Formulas

Max Heart Rate (MHR): 220 – Age = MHR or 208 – (0.7 x Age) = MHR
e.g. 30 year old would have Max HR of 190 BPM | 220 – 30 = 190 BPM

Heart Rate Reserve (HRR): Max HR – Resting HR = HRR
e.g. 30 year old with resting HR of 60 BPM | 190 - 60 = 130 BPM

Target Heart Rate (THR) = HRR x % Intensity + Resting HR **(Karvonen Formula)**
e.g. 30 year old mentioned above to train at 80% intensity | 130 x 0.80 + 60 = 164 BPM (THR)

Body Mass Index (BMI) = Weight (Kg) ÷ Height (m^2)
e.g. calculate the BMI of a man who is 6ft tall & weighs 180 pounds
180 ÷ 2.2 = 81.81 Kg | 6ft x 12 = 72 inches |72 x 2.54 = 182.88 cm | 182.88 ÷ 100 = 1.83 m
|1.83m^2 = 3.35 | 81.81 ÷ 3.35 = 24.42 BMI

Fat weight (FW) = Body weight (BW) x Body fat (BF) %
e.g. calculate based on 180 pound body weight & 20% body fat | 180 x 0.20 = 36 lbs of fat

Lean body weight (LBW) = Body weight (BW) – Fat weight (FW)
e.g. calculate based on information above | 180 – 36 = 144 lbs LBW

Desired Body Weight (DBW) = Lean body weight ÷ (100% - Desired body fat %)
e.g. calculate DBW if the person above wanted to be at 10% body fat | 144 ÷ 0.90 = 160 lbs

Waist to Hip Ratio (WHR) = Waist circumference ÷ Hip circumference
e.g. calculate based on an individual with a 32-inch waist and 36-inch hip | 32 ÷ 36 = 0.89

Areas of Focus

The following are the major areas to focus on while reviewing the material learned:

* Objective and Subjective Assessments *(know the difference)*

* Progressions and Regressions *(know for common exercises)*

* Spotting and Cueing Techniques *(know appropriate cues)*

* Muscle Locations and Names by Area of Body

* Muscle Imbalances and Postural Distortion Patterns

* Overactive and Underactive Muscles Involved in Imbalances.

* The OPT Model and Associated Phases

* Flexibility Continuum *(SMR, Static, Active-Isolated, Dynamic)*

Practice Questions

1) Which of the following cognitive-behavioral approaches helps to increase a client's accountability and program adherence?

    A. Association
    B. Self-talk
    C. Self-monitoring
    D. Dissociation

2) The force-couple relationship is best described by which of the following?

    A. The contraction of one muscle and the relaxation of its antagonist.
    B. Muscle groups moving together to produce movement around a joint.
    C. Detect differences in tension within a muscle.
    D. The ability to return to normal or resting length after being stretched.

3) _____ states that soft tissue will align along the lines of stress that are placed upon it.

    A. Durnin-Womersley formula
    B. Vertical loading
    C. Linear Periodization
    D. Davis's Law

4) A fitness professional notices their client's arms falling forward during an overhead squat assessment. What muscles are likely overactive?

    A. Latissimus Dorsi, Pectoral muscles
    B. Rhomboids, Rotator cuff
    C. Mid & Lower Trapezius
    D. Gluteus Maximus & Medius

5) Which of the following correctly describes a SMART goal?

    A. "I want to lose weight before my vacation this summer."
    B. "I want to be strong enough to perform an unassisted pull-up."
    C. "I want to lose 20 pounds before my friend's wedding in 3 months."
    D. "I want to gain 10 pounds of lean muscle this month."

6) What stage of change is a person in who works out on occasion but has recently decided to hire a personal trainer and exercise on a regular basis?

    A. Maintenance
    B. Action
    C. Pre-contemplation
    D. Preparation

7) What position should a pregnant woman avoid during exercise after the 1st trimester?

    A. Supine
    B. Prone
    C. Lateral
    D. Medial

8) Which of the following exercises involves triple extension of the pivot leg?

    A. Single leg squat touchdown
    B. Medicine ball lift & chop
    C. Single leg romanian deadlift
    D. Multiplanar lunges

9) Marie is a 35-year-old with a resting heart rate of 50 BPM. What would her target heart rate be if she is looking to train at 80% intensity of her Heart Rate Reserve (HRR)?

    A. 148 BPM
    B. 153 BPM
    C. 158 BPM
    D. 151 BPM

10) Gathering a client's medical history is an example of which type of assessment?

    A. Objective assessment
    B. Pre-assessment
    C. Cardiorespiratory assessment
    D. Subjective assessment

11) Which postural distortion syndrome is characterized by a forward head and rounded shoulders?

    A. Pronation distortion syndrome
    B. Upper crossed syndrome
    C. Proprioception syndrome
    D. Lower crossed syndrome

12) The _____ states that in order to create physiological changes an exercise stimulus must be applied at an intensity greater than the body is accustomed to receiving.

    A. Principle of specificity
    B. FITTE principle
    C. Principle of variation
    D. Overload principle

13) Static stretching is used during the _____ phase of flexibility training.

    A. Active flexibility
    B. Corrective flexibility
    C. Functional flexibility
    D. Relative flexibility

14) What is an appropriate progression once a client can successfully perform a single-leg squat?

    A. Single-leg squat on balance pad
    B. Two-leg squat
    C. Single-leg deadlift
    D. Two-leg squat on Dyna disc

15) The lowering portion of a squat is considered the _____ phase of the movement.

    A. Isometric
    B. Concentric
    C. Eccentric
    D. Dynamic

16) A person is considered obese when their BMI meets or exceeds which of the following numbers?

    A. 25
    B. 30
    C. 20
    D. 40

17) What is an appropriate spotting technique when a client is performing an overhead dumbbell press?

    A. Spotting at the elbows of the client through a full range of motion.
    B. Taking the weight from the client once they begin to struggle.
    C. Helping client through any *"sticking point"* while spotting at the wrists.
    D. Keeping hands on the weight while the client performs the exercise.

18) Performing cardio at 76-85% of HR_{Max} falls into which cardiorespiratory training zone?

    A. Zone 1
    B. Zone 2
    C. Zone 3
    D. Recovery

19) What is the primary energy system used during explosive power movements such as sprinting and jumping?

    A. ATP-PC
    B. Oxidative
    C. Glycolytic
    D. Aerobic

20) Which of the following is an example of an objective assessment?

    A. Medical history
    B. Past hypertension
    C. Resting heart rate
    D. Current stage of change

21) Which of the following cues should a trainer give to a client whose knees are caving in during a squat exercise?

    A. "Internally rotate your feet."
    B. "Keep your knees in line with your second toe."
    C. "Externally rotate your feet."
    D. "Keep your knees in line with your shoulders."

22) What is an appropriate regression for a client's whose lumbo-pelvic hip complex (LPHC) is unstable while performing prone-iso abs (plank)?

    A. Side plank
    B. Single-leg plank
    C. Quadruped drawing in maneuver
    D. Plank with feet on a bench

23) Muscles that act primarily as stabilizers generally contain greater concentrations of which type of muscle fibers?

    A. Type I (slow-twitch)
    B. Type IIx (fast-twitch)
    C. Type IIa (intermediate)
    D. Muscle spindles

24) Which chamber of the heart is responsible for collecting deoxygenated blood from the body?

    A. Right ventricle
    B. Left ventricle
    C. Right atrium
    D. Left atrium

25) A client who is performing ice skaters is training in which phase of the OPT Model?

    A. Phase 1 (Stabilization Endurance)
    B. Phase 5 (Power)
    C. Phase 4 (Maximal Strength)
    D. Phase 3 (Hypertrophy)

26) Excess post-exercise oxygen consumption (EPOC) causes _____ following exercise.

A. A decrease in metabolism
B. An elevated heart rate
C. A decreased heart rate
D. Elevated metabolism

27) Which training format describes working different muscle groups on separate days?

A. Superset
B. Periodization
C. Split-routine
D. Circuit training

28) What are the recommended hold times for each of the following stretching techniques: Self-myofascial release (SMR), Static, and Active-Isolated?

A. SMR (20 seconds) / Static (30 seconds) / Active-isolated (1-2 seconds)
B. SMR (30 seconds) / Static (30 seconds) / Active-isolated (3-5 seconds)
C. SMR (30 seconds) / Static (30 seconds) / Active-isolated (1-2 seconds)
D. SMR (30 seconds) / Static (20 seconds) / Active-isolated (3-5 seconds)

29) Which of the following medications causes a decrease in heart rate & blood pressure?

A. Antidepressants
B. Beta-blockers
C. Vasodilators
D. Nitrates

30) What underactive muscles should be strengthened if a client's shoulders elevate during pushing & pulling assessments?

A. Mid & lower trapezius
B. Latissimus dorsi
C. Upper trapezius
D. Sternocleidomastoid

31) A fitness professional should have and maintain adequate _____ prior to working with clients.

   A. Testing forms
   B. Meal plans
   C. Liability insurance
   D. Health-history questionnaires

32) In what plane of motion does an overhead shoulder press occur?

   A. Frontal
   B. Sagittal
   C. Transverse
   D. Vertical

33) What is an appropriate amount of rest when performing circuit training in Phase 5 of the OPT Model?

   A. 1 – 2 minutes
   B. 3 – 5 minutes
   C. 60 – 90 seconds
   D. 0 – 30 seconds

34) A fitness professional should refer a client to a licensed medical professional when they become aware of which of the following?

   A. Diagnosed hypertension.
   B. An undiagnosed injury.
   C. Diagnosed diabetes.
   D. DOMS (Delayed Onset Muscle Soreness)

35) What is the recommended total set range in a given workout to provide adequate stimulus while also helping to prevent overtraining?

   A. 12 - 24
   B. 44 - 58
   C. 24 - 36
   D. 36 - 48

36) What muscle action follows the eccentric loading phase during the vertical jump test?

    A. Isometric

    B. Concentric

    C. Dynamic

    D. Isokinetic

37) Which of the following is an example of a reactive strength exercise?

    A. Single-leg squat touchdown

    B. Tuck jumps

    C. Multiplanar lunge to balance

    D. Ice skaters

38) What type of flexibility training should be used during a warm-up in the power phase of the OPT Model?

    A. Active flexibility

    B. Relative flexibility

    C. Corrective flexibility

    D. Functional flexibility

39) A client's lower back begins to arch while performing push-ups. What is an appropriate cue to help correct their form?

    A. "Elevate your hips."

    B. "Brace your core."

    C. "Look straight ahead."

    D. "Stabilize your shoulders."

40) _____ describes the simultaneous contraction of one muscle and the relaxation of its antagonist to allow movement to take place.

    A. Autogenic inhibition

    B. Proprioception

    C. Reciprocal inhibition

    D. Synergistic dominance

41) The purpose of the Davies test is to assess which of the following?

    A. Lower body strength and power
    B. Upper extremity agility and stabilization
    C. Lower extremity agility and neuromuscular control
    D. Upper body strength and endurance

42) What should a fitness professional obtain before training a client with a diagnosed cardiorespiratory disease?

    A. Medical clearance
    B. Informed consent
    C. Liability waiver
    D. PAR-Q form

43) What muscles are likely overactive if a client's feet turn out during an overhead squat assessment?

    A. Anterior & Posterior Tibialis
    B. Gluteus Maximus & Medius
    C. Soleus & Lateral Gastrocnemius
    D. Pectoralis Major & Minor

44) Which of the following would primarily work the oxidative energy system?

    A. Sprinting
    B. Plyometric circuit training.
    C. Maximal strength training. *(low reps, high intensity)*
    D. 30 minutes of steady state cardio on an elliptical machine.

45) What is an appropriate starting point for a client who is obese and very deconditioned?

    A. Begin by performing single sets and progress to multiple sets once their conditioning improves.
    B. Begin with High-Intensity Interval Training *(HIIT)* to improve their conditioning.
    C. Begin with only single-joint exercises to prevent excessive fatigue.
    D. Begin with dynamic balance and reactive exercises to improve their neuromuscular efficiency.

46) What is the FIRST step a fitness professional should take if they come across a person lying unconscious in the locker room?

   A. Perform CPR immediately
   B. Locate the first aid kit & AED.
   C. Check the area for hazards
   D. Activate the emergency response system (EMS)

47) Two friends have joined a group fitness class together. They encourage each other to keep going as they prepare for a summer vacation. What type of support are they providing each other?

   A. Intrinsic support
   B. Social support
   C. Emotional support
   D. Extrinsic support

48) Which type of training is the preferred method used in the power level (Phase 5) of the OPT Model?

   A. Peripheral Heart Action System (PHA)
   B. High-Intensity Interval Training (HIIT)
   C. Superset
   D. Hypertrophy

49) Which of the following helps to improve neuromuscular efficiency?

   A. Horizontal loading
   B. Proprioceptively enriched environments
   C. Vertical loading
   D. Metabolic conditioning circuit

50) What is occurring when the hamstrings take on the work of the gluteus maximus?

   A. Altered reciprocal inhibition
   B. Autogenic inhibition
   C. Synergistic dominance
   D. Integrated function

Practice Question Answers

1) **C** / Self-monitoring

2) **B** / Muscle groups moving together to produce movement around a joint.

3) **D** / Davis's Law

4) **A** / Latissimus Dorsi, Pectoral muscles

5) **C** / "I want to lose 20 pounds before my friend's wedding in 3 months." / This goal meets all of the requirements of a SMART goal: Specific, Measurable, Attainable, Realistic, and Time-bound.

6) **D** / Preparation / This person is in the preparation stage because they have made plans to exercise on a regular basis but are not currently doing so. The **action** stage is when a person has been exercising regularly but for **less than 6 months**. The **maintenance** stage is when a person has been exercising regularly for **6 months or more**.

7) **A** / Supine

8) **B** / Medicine ball lift & chop / Involves plantarflexion of the foot and extension of the hip and knee *(triple extension)*.

9) **C** / 158 BPM | Target Heart Rate = Max HR - Resting HR x % of Intensity + Resting HR
220-35 = 185 Max Heart Rate | 185-50 x 0.80 + 50 = 158 BPM

10) **D** / Subjective assessment / Used to obtain information about a client's personal history, as well as his or her occupation, lifestyle, and medical background.

11) **B** / Upper crossed syndrome

12) **D** / Overload principle

13) **B** / Corrective flexibility

14) **D** / Two-leg squat on Dyna disc / Appropriate balance progressions are as follows: Two-leg stable, single-leg stable, two-leg unstable, single-leg unstable.

15) **C** / Eccentric

16) **B** / 30

17) **C** / Helping client through any *"sticking point"* while spotting at the wrists. / It's important to spot at the wrists when a client is performing dumbbell exercises to help them maintain control of weight as necessary.

18) **B** / Zone 2 / Cardiorespiratory training zones are as follows: Zone 1 (65-75% of HR_{Max}) / Zone 2 (76-85% of HR_{Max}) / Zone 3 (86-95% of HR_{Max})

19) **A** / ATP-PC / This is the immediate short-term energy system that utilizes the ATP stored in muscle. The ATP-PC system is primarily used for explosive and maximal strength type movements such as sprinting and Olympic style power lifts.

20) **C** / Resting heart rate / **Objective assessment**: Assessment that addresses observations that can be directly measured and quantified by the fitness professional. *(Resting heart rate, Blood pressure, Posture and movement assessments)*

21) **B** / "Keep your knees in line with your second toe."

22) **C** / Quadruped drawing in maneuver

23) **A** / Type I *(slow-twitch)* / Stabilizer muscles contain greater concentrations of Type-1 *(slow-twitch)* muscle fibers which are better suited for endurance.

24) **C** / Right atrium / The right atrium is responsible for collecting deoxygenated blood coming from the body, and the right ventricle pumps this blood through the lungs. The left atrium collects the oxygenated blood from the lungs, and the left ventricle pumps it to all parts of the body.

25) **B** / Phase 5 (Power)

26) **D** / Elevated metabolism

27) **C** / Split-routine

28) **C** / SMR (30 seconds) / Static (30 seconds) / Active-isolated (1-2 seconds) / Holding SMR & static stretches for at least 30 seconds allows the Golgi tendon organs (GTO) to cause autogenic inhibition of the muscle and a relaxation response.

29) **B** / Beta-blockers

30) **A** / Mid & lower trapezius

31) **C** / Liability insurance

32) **A** / Frontal

33) **B** / 3 – 5 minutes

34) **B** / An undiagnosed injury

35) **C** / 24 – 36 / Performing more than 36 total sets within a workout increases the chance of overtraining.

36) **A** / Isometric / **Integrated performance paradigm (stretch-shortening cycle)**: A forceful cycle of muscle contraction that involves eccentric loading of the muscle, isometric muscle contraction *(amortization phase)*, and concentric muscle contraction.

37) **B** / Tuck jumps

38) **D** / Functional flexibility / Includes SMR and Dynamic stretching that helps prepare the body for the power training that follows.

39) **B** / "Brace your core" *(abdominal bracing cue)*

40) **C** / Reciprocal inhibition

41) **B** / Upper extremity agility and stabilization

42) **A** / Medical clearance

43) **C** / Soleus & Lateral Gastrocnemius

44) **D** / 30 minutes of steady state cardio on an elliptical machine / The oxidative energy system requires oxygen to produce ATP and predominates with sustained physical activity lasting longer than 2 minutes.

45) **A** / Begin by performing single sets and progress to multiple sets once their conditioning improves.

46) **C** / Check the area for hazards / This is the first step in the CPR protocol.

47) **B** / Social support

48) **C** / Superset / Combining a maximal strength exercise immediately followed by an explosive power exercise for the same muscle group to increase overall muscular power.

49) **B** / Proprioceptively enriched environments / e.g. dumbbell chest press on stability ball

50) **C** / Synergistic dominance / When synergists take over function for weak or inhibited prime movers.

Thank You!

We want to thank you for choosing our study guide to help prepare for the NASM CPT Exam. It is truly gratifying to share some insight & help you along your journey as a fitness professional. If you found value in the content provided we would appreciate a review expressing your thoughts by following the link below.

 http://www.amazon.com/gp/product-reviews/B071R6N5T8

~ CPT Exam Prep Team

Visit our website below for additional insights or to message us with any questions you may have while preparing for your exam.

www.cptprep.com
Follow us on social @CPTPrep

Contact via e-mail at info@cptprep.com
Your feedback is welcomed and appreciated!

<u>References</u>

1) NASM Essentials of Personal Fitness Training *(Sixth Edition)*.

Made in the USA
San Bernardino, CA
16 August 2018